OLVIDOS
JOHN M. BENNETT

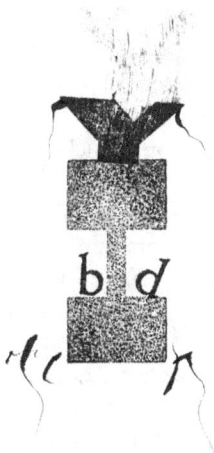

LUNA BISONTE PRODS
2013

OLVIDOS

© John M. Bennett 2013

April-October 2012

*For All My Bennetts,
and Especially for C. Mehrl Bennett*

Title page and p. 340 rubber stamp/calligraphy: John M. Bennett
Front and back cover visual poems: John M. Bennett
Back cover photo: Jeff Sass
Book and cover design: C. Mehrl Bennett

Some these poems have been previously published, sometimes in different form, in the following excellent publications:
Otoliths, Caliban Online, E.Ratio, Blank Sight/Naked Sunfish, 48th St. Press Broadsides, Franticham's Assembling Box, Haiku Canada Review, Eccolinguistics, Altered Scale, The Altered Scale Blog, Pense Agui, Open World, Fluxus Porn, Experiential-Experimental-Literature, La Factoría Barroca, Apricot Blossom, Truck, GAR, Liberté: In the Shadow of the 19th Century, KART, Mailart Makes the World a Town, On Barcelona, Bizarre Cities, Expoesía Visual Experimental, Cricket Online Review; in the following TLPs from Luna Bisonte Prods: Olvidos del White Verse Urine, 6 Olvidos 6, Ebircs, Mute Soap [with C. Mehrl Bennett], Pooeh; and in these chapbooks: Olvidos del Perú, Rockhampton, Australia: Otoliths, 2012 [Otoliths, issue 27, part 3], and Olvidos de Chile, in Blank Sight/Naked Sunfish, 72, 2012. Some of the poems were performed by Bennett, Luis Bravo, and Jon Cone on the audio work AREÑAL, forthcoming in Montevideo, Uruguay, and Columbus, Ohio.

ISBN: 978-1-938521-05-8

LUNA BISONTE PRODS
137 Leland Ave.
Columbus, OH 43214 USA

www.johnmbennett.net
http://www.lulu.com/spotlight/lunabisonteprods

OLVIDOS
John M. Bennett

olvido
   - for Nicolas Carras

scra wl the turd leaf)turd
sh ape st icky pa vement cig
butt rising on the grease ah
))p ink p aper)))folding o
pen answer maybe in the b
anana pee l your t
issue))))turd ,con
crete ,plas tick c up
)))))turd))))))nothing
(((((((birds creaking
far a way

olvido

nase oall oodrunken b oom
cl aimed c lam n eck to
replasm)s hape craw
ling down the f loor ne
ver d rank the))shut nor
)))eminencia cave ooosea
deal ,log sh ape))))s
ink inside the clou d ome
oooothumping shirt a ,cl
one b log)))))easer p
ill the ,glass half oooootan
tan el vidrio))))))sin fin
,comido ooooola mitad com
ida)))))))eats a way
the ooooooo louder nostril

olvido

dog drink ,mile ,O clang beet
burned ,the ,ink dick f
olded in your snore shorts
OO dimes rivered beneath
the bed your corn heel
my socks arf OOO dune
the temple OOOO drifts
ají yr eye in sleeps OO
OOO)*burning room*( )I
p lunged(neck id r
,aw fog lit OOOOOO be
neath]the cash lint[o
come a OOOOOOO nd d
rain yr comOOOOOOOments
in yr liver fermentation

olvido

chew an gn ash the lun g f
art *f* matter grunty wh
ere my *ff* h air ch eese
e)cto))murphic *fff* wa*ll*
dims)))me atless sh
ffff irt roollling in the
fffff dust))))jum py
,bu bb led c rag f lies a
h *ffffff* lame *ffffff*
lag ga gging on the cl iff
,you ,corne red ,dogfield
u)))))tter lam ination
)*ffffffff*)))))ace sp
linter writ ten on yr
*fffff*ton*ffff*gue g*ue* g

olvido

mint to L ap poration tor
n orre LL pizzing inna
LLL cor ner the che
wy brot h ⊓⊓)c rime(
)mota muerta(pi LLLL
ake rising in my pants t
he tousLedL*LLL* h and of
see ds)shoo ting(ton
guelock LLLLLL]eat
the b omb re ad f
oot in the dark ,bajo
la me sa *LLLLLLL*
la nad a ví la na da
da na da mp shor ne
socks ay e vap or a
tio*nnnnnnnn* . . . .

olvido

noose *s* jump sore lugar
ss eething d rip d ream *sss*
matter an my m ortal l
eash *ssss* f ray *sssss* g
uttered deck resis tance
an my cornbelt fog ⊓⊓⊓ *s*
sssss))the roots(( ))roll((
drug the leg *sss s sss* yr
lisp dominion jassssssssper
ssssssssskull sp lashing in
yr Inka Kola)tzompantli
pegajoso(sssssssss the
lake with snakes was
roiling clouds th
ickened in your heads *th*
e a nts ~ ~ ~ ~   ~   ~   ~

olvido

*suit ,)))))))time thirst ,ek
phasis stammer))))))sho rt
of s tock my shaking tic k
the cru ets d rip)))))phone
watch er the crowncloud pul
sates on yr screen))))aver
age inches pages [] to wer in
the ...s.....and............ m utte
ring in the*)))mouthpiece
,like a grittty ddrink .my
namefog giggles my ran
cid sleeve my dribbbling h
eel))*less time than d
og nor more than*)whis
tles ,*the bushes smoulder*(((((((

olvido

where the crippled lake dou
bles driedd my bleat tune
dddoubt spam beliveredddd
shipwise ,metereddddd in the
coffee *I was on the cramping
chair I was lifting off that*
dddddddog grime swivel tur
neddddddd that blotto sp
oon)*my mouth reception*(
conjuntibitus ,gnat con
tusion ,blinky shaddddddddow
scrambler ,ape of ate
."knelt upon the shore" the
crawled explanation dddd
dddddid I thunderstand
dddddidddd I know the
air was drinking

olvido

*ww*hen the *ww*indow gas ex
haled your tomb yr eau re
did the inch if ruled a
posture *wwww*atered like
a *wwwww*hip o regodeo
ornitológico lo que nada
eres *wwwwww*allet ingresado
en lo ,empírico ,ninsensato
,foggy *wwwwwww*avered was
,the hamstrings greased the
*wwwwwww*andered lon
tananza ffilled with ffumes
]gutters ,nodding[the aging

rafters *wwwwwwww***W**atch
"was creaking in your sleep"

olvido

hush ounce ,taste lather rip,ply
endblock[the lungish phone wh
eeze)zzipper))laszzzt ,the
dingus suit surely shunted to
my flaparoscopic zzzzstung l
eash .pulmonar ,endocóptico
,ru tilante ni la zzzzzonafísica
de mis tuercas tuertas)))*f
ound my loose*))))chaw
beaker ,zzzzzz its no
dding in the scrumbled p
ages where my hock shirt
crawls su)))))titubeo zz
zzzzzingular))))))mi *sue
ño múltiple*((((((

olvido

dik dik ,¿dónde? tornillo in
ttonso *rest ahead* chow slottt
.ttthe slacks bile y puse
el lomo ,platttto de hule
,*lo singular ni gula* es res
tttittutiva mi cáscara ,ttt
ttttrueno 4 the raucous
ttttimerfartttt shape re
amer ,*"amargo el aire"* ins
ttttantttáneo mi Túnel
liberado yr mmutttturd
leg g g ¡ay ,mi gritttto o
grifo!))surely the shirtttt
was coughing in the sttreett((
T

olvido

som bral ,intimista ,cha
in sucker flab flabber s
ate the crunx soaps to
mbbb]seals[ ]shot door[
en raizal en tubbbb métrico
las casas de cartón ,em
papadas el sueño sin
bbbbbólido ,*stock the fine
collapse* the streaming
window bbbbbboils with r
age an nubbbbbbbes del
desespertar my soil sh
adow "seemed" ronq
uido sorta ,the libbbbbbbbp
speedch *labial que
era* ,tumbefacta como
tormentalengua **Sieze the
Shirt**

olvido

wh ite lake bod y
et ic y cla y b ooks
ra in ;;; ;;;; ; ; ; see n
ho use puzz le gend
dus t teas roo f d
ying bi g cam us sq
uiggly woof ,bur ied
mou th re members
the nam es s tore un
conscious def inition en
tered sir en's con tent
pi si de *d u s t*

Evaporated from Ivan Argüelles'
"puzzling" & (education)

olvido

net("clalm" mouthed pants
leg wrink led((twist er
peel(((dog an leak ,mi
me the rust ling corn er L
s peeds ,k notty nor th
ought (((( )*itch*(cl
aimed the is thmus lin
ed with doors[[[[
)d ragging the cloud c
over tongued s treet sh
irtless moo n slo bbing
in the cul verts ra
coon skull blooming rock
et *toi l'oeil fotolacustre*

olvido

was sneezing in the corn was
.son sobado ,returned .cap
sule faced a)head dingk
.)"named a floor")swell
an)door c lutter ,nos
tril in my n ape)your
)cheese grasp ,deep twit
,muscled)knee or negck
)pollen on the l eaves w
hat form lies down)c
hew the)stone robado
)learned)the bread ,my
)fl utter last breath)"my"
.(((((((((((((

olvido

news mi caca bore mi
tumbaronda ,lapsos inco
ordinados let me .aging
taste the stone verdusca
,salsa fulminante es mi
,trono ,cacaficante ,res
tive shadow ,silly ,tor
qued outside the wall
et ,was ininpensable
,stuffed with forks o
senderos difurcantes I
ate my noticiero and ate
it again mi noticia de
agua en llamas spiraling
down the ,plughole *b
right with ahspirina*

olvido

dense desk captive toodt maker
shades ,bum or ,loot twaddle
,same nor least of leakers
.en gate swarm ,plause
,neh forks ,shot ,with
tunnels ,gasoline an rages
.tunnel the spackled
leaf saw read saw
red and numb ered
in the b lack of rugless
,eyes ,of stink of
,swelling gates in ah
foggy sun ay be es *qui*
vering in my shoe

olvido

dot luster nor ,pelted ,came
the sewer ,nipper past
,the "redhead jap" skull
king down the ,alley la
ced with glowing t rash
,soaked the dream net ,b
louse blackened in the fot
o ni sípida es mi cu
spidora shapely like
,a gnewt if ,chasing
,creamed be side the
lagunilla ,redonda y ho
nda como mi *b⬤ca*
hablacagada

olvido

number shape ,clod goal each
distancerage ,what gravel
,was ashed ,if counted not
a ,burning in the g lade of
,garbage and old TVs
my chair ,limp an twisty
,leaning in the ,where corn
,field ,I sat in not
,walking ,b lazed the in
stance with a ,blanker
,tombstone and my title
.if was gates was ,ton
gued ,but dry ,the sandy
stone .my walk ,nor lad
dered ,wrestled with a tree

olvido

¿ne ck ¿dust ¿lip ¿ash
ham per me ate s the treet a
ir my stinging foot sp
ire ??less dim sheet less
???slime meal , pink the p
untos sus pensivos ????sh
it's ,doorway in your sou
nd // c lack ,shover ,s
aw the frog puzzle's f
?????loppy c hunks ,s k y
window ,the ,loss chained
,the d ,amp zipper the
??????)churning caminata
...............toward the leap /   /   /
●)●)●)*potatos tumbling off the c/*
iff

olvido

duck sot ,mime mat ecto
lymphic ,echo ,meal ,p
ry the cap shot off ,y
our quack shine nes
tles ou,ter seenfog
lit inside a ,wrassled
toad a tomb .buzzed
,clotted ,negato wr
eathed yr ,up shat and
,talked the bread off
.nine samples addled
,mortíferos ,niluminados
,ectomórficos like yr
shitshine Ay the be
ak wavered in yr w
indow !pulmonito ,h
uff for me . . .   .   .

olvido

pu// the p/ug no wise s
tocker swo// pestive sh
it/eaks bor n into what as
pha/t mimewrap b/aze the
care of /ymph stones ay
piecer stink con so/idation
where the bath s/ows d own I
counted the single carrot tw
ice mind three ,/eaf/ess
,spraying towe/s ,loosely
/abia/ where my phage
ref/ection /eft the g/ass
*]towering down])baited
,g/and ,dogged gu//et(* **w
here my water shines**

olvido

muy hosed bossed dunce cr
eature ,fails to w rinkle do
pler senda lops before the
gate sorda ,drinking ,fal
tered que muere ,turned w
ay in lo mismo ,vascular
an ahogada sung my so
pping sleeves lo que ron
co libero puts the jefe
*plowed mine eyen across
the field* ,en mi la za
nahoria única es ,un
olvido de su túnel lleno
pass the p late an squat
down on the *steps*

olvido

the low sty swims no hay
nada lamps condense la
nada hay un tugurio
flooded with my breathing
en la nada nula ,nom
bre swollen with a
corner sleep la nada h
ay festival an lu
ggage swarmed to st
ink an grin o lake na
dar what lesser deck's
what nods the nada nor
was nada en la nada
jumping from the gnats
swirling in my shorts

olvido

the pulsing corn was needled
in yr ampulation was
that crawling dial a cross
the bedroom where the
mumbled sheet was so
aking in a corner like the
blood a sandwich mum
bled tape your elbow to
the toilet lid an shad
ow all your books with
cheese ay kernels doub
led in the loot my
accujuncture !halllight
sweating where the
aperture **o o o o o o**

olvido

tepid cake
my shirred fork

towel

olvido

y nunca me
lo re
cor dé

)o exprimir(

olvido

*,fog ,shake ,tool
,risen ,lake*

]plow[

olvido

nunca supe nun
ca mino

big s p a c e

)the last dog(

olvido

my snore
my loss
my

;r;a;i;n; ; bus
)iness(

olvido

deeper neck

flame

risen glue

"*glueless*"

olvido

went to
dog

the pile the mile

olvido

rat **I** said **I**

"sizzled"

))*in the cloud***((**

olvido

bull et
mistère

baulk me

"the stunning peel"

olvido

sere should
not wiggle
nor the knee
my pluster
fat cod
went nor waved

olvido

deep
neck
droll
seen

)check(

the crowd

olvido

soft blood
my tune
muscle corn
sure fuzz
sure
meat

no

olvido

built a nom
lo innombrable
seen was
the fucking sort

shutters

olvido

off the lake in
tempestive
the balcón creeping

wheat

olvido

lost door lint lung lint *w i n d*
luz licuada mi lumbre libre ca
ga tum ba la tu erca el lo mo the
lumpy length you twisted ne
ver mind the ,seen sugar ti
me towel an my ,*your tumb*
bled shoe fumes beneath the
bed ah glossy snore ah bent
daze sung an loose !the
bark house the next door the
roots' dark garlic the
scalded luminescence in your
shirtless pocket ay breath an
limp limp mumbler in your
trouser leg the *talking air*

olvido

rent truster an the dogger
led the ,leg counts ,blew a
crunk yr sam shirter ,est
nur plendy la corona nad
aficante la palabra "the" a
toda madre y la puerta se
alquila .don Luis ahogada en
su mar *avec les bergères* my
wallet vacant with a
bag of rice of worms of
gravel sparkling in the
alley O yr sucking hat
O ~ ~   )*loosing blood*   )wal
k away   )*the shingled mon*

//◉\\

olvido

t here was nnot hing nnut a
,pplungged gas wrin kkle
,aimedd ,norr pto maine
gloww a ,leakking be
astt ay mystère que
shhadowwedd !*pawingg*
throughh the ggreasy d
doorr wrungg clouud
my "phasial incognition"
it'ss a ntool itt's .a
ggutt mind a ,rinnse
my ffeet .yr a
gging laddder ,notte
boogks fulla clogcks a
bugcket of filtthy clotth

olvido

mi sobaco nimio tu fo
nología ñoña "leper"
or "casita" shapewant
,the clanking washcloth w
here yr dark conconclusion
wrote yr itchy back I
ate riñones drank a lag
o *flat an grey the morning
sleep* _ _ _ _ _ _ _ _ _ o _ _ _

))endémico mi fin o tierra en
terrada mi fango fiscal y
sudadera *aatmosféérica*   *a*

olvido

wind-germ empire sand
hisses Urpayhuachac furiosa
lo persiguió includes snow
shadows layer logic una
gran peña hizo crecer marks
fish seen encolerizado los
arrojó todos al mar fork
deluge light travelled tone
clocks huacas locales slippery
business clothes sabiendo
que el mar soon disappears
reality if decisions iba a
desbordar their square
window que se ennegreció
nearby events trajectory las
piedras indeterminate trans
formations se golpearon unas
memories con otras raw
multiplicity no hacían otra
cosa social contrast que
guerrear haphazard time
restric cinco huevos un solo
hombre permax rectional
means effecting unspoken
subió al cerro manifestation
discourse ephemeral structure
allí se adormeció here to
gether downspout una ser
piente vive encima reflect

body rarity cultural artifacts
por haber fingido emblematic
ser dios abandoned se puso
furioso collapses revolutionary
agency interior spiral un
sapo con dos cabezas
homeopathic history la mujer
gritó hears nothing decorated
the cave change space el
viento no había aparecido
delivers a belief room te
echarás a volar across the
privacy la tierra tembló
without amplification laws
never begins al día siguiente
sin sentido such as rots se
convirtió en piedra like a
horse blazing flea re
ligion la colocó boca
abajo en el suelo
sweat and fingernails había
de ser comida rejection
para los hombres poetry
parking mientras bailaban
una cachua memory pro
tocol shopping los arras
traron foam milk eyes
hacia el mar restless
swerve destruction solía
comerse a los hombres
violent absurd cloud

barrage flmuddle sighit
matarte también power
controls changing socks
para regar las chacras
horizontal mi maicita
unimaginable la acequia
bluish fires flux
Huarochirí tactile shoe
convulsion creeds suits
arts vulture a es
condidas una granizada
stem narrative apparatus
phony commitment desire ¿a
dónde vas llorando así?
icon book en el primer
capítulo dimensional
games solía comer
shifts serpes pyramid
carne humana wrapped
el aliento cardboard
salía de su boca

From Jim Leftwich's
Six Months Aint No Sentence, Book 20, 2012
&
Ritos y Tradiciones de Huarochirí, [ca. 1609],
versión [de] Gerald Taylor, Lima: Instituto de
Estudios Peruanos, 1987.

olvido

trot torn lake la tumba sor
da por el zumo camin aba c
on un pez de p lata o platero era l
ot was born my "fake mile" sl
athered with yr }*toothache*{ sky
damp thing wres tled))soup((
inch was ,las toallas rascadas
,si quemadas son ,ascuas y
lumen race the forks an *p*
lease creeper ,nesteds ,pas
t the sop ventana crusts of
,scalp rudder ,times of ,"d
ay" coiled un coi ,en el vi
ento muerto algo ,que "dormía"
,un fútil era ,útil por el a
gua pibil para senda es
camada ,))*mi cuate*((((((

olvido

siempre rutil ante mano ,soco
rrido no me sismo you but t
akes the rlabbit spplutters
cake against the glass un tr
ueno es .pues hombre ,fus
ilánime ,sudorificante como n
ada ,nodding ,nadante en
la tazajante cafetero .me
vi la palabrisa inescrita ,al
go en la palma ,algas sin
sentido que entendía lo que
supe ,sé .say or .sp
read whirrled writ the
nube nexo the lomo a
hogado con sus caras in
finitas derretidas y los
dedos desintegr *antes que*
me asen a toda muerte

olvido

nada había ni ,una lluvia frágil
,nube de concreto ,o de concreto
nube ,numbered ,necked my
shadow ,louder ladder c
rashed into the glass my
restive leather contur
bado seats and skies the
,shiny splinters con mis
reflejos surely ,yes a
something hair ,nuca nu
nca mas ,an ear an air
.field cloud ,gnat luck
,dog piled and ,forma tu
erca ,y puerca mi
cara o calle o ,climbed
,up an out ,the strips of
shadow laid out in rows
,and *ffluttterredd d d   d   d*

:::::f:::o::g:::::::::::::::

olvido

tuca tuca .sent drown ,ma p
ile ah, smoulders an my
shiphole ,spewlls ,the wadd
led corn soaked my hat
hot .western bowel ,el in
odoro ,musa y plectrum
,took and took my ,bent
clown's damp ,*shoulder*
,knew I'm born .a louder
shit time my))blast d((
oom o eggs of plate con
salsa ,fin indextro ,la
ruta caca ,su dor mir
ror "shapely" inna cama
where mis *hüevos th*
ink their gruel

olvido

p lot *p* lunge nec k my
sore shoe luncher ,wings the
bio had *I held my* .each fog
nudge each ,felafel sand
wich blOod an boOm eye
the coldcuts ,*where the s* tink
ling where the mum blur whe
re my *toilet stuffed with
books* the lake floor d
rains no end .nor start
led pageant where my sh
ouldered drizzle loomed
yr seen corn stool uh he
aven's sock coiling *do
wn the wall*

olvido

the lid
run
basement

fetal wind

olvido

my dents
my
my
sealed luster
gas in
ta
te *text*
in

olvido

- for Blaster Al Ackerman

his nutty neck hi
s lacker tr ack gum
my comb b ending in
his pocket thorns and
coins es *gringo de pura
cepa* wading through a
garlic patch a st
inkbug rides' pants a
a llongg ttappper sp
pillinng cofffee "chch
oose the ssttorm you
ssttummble in"))the
batthroom where a g
gleaming((ththird
way ggullps arround
his ththronèd bbutt
o o o o o   o
o "his nuts on neck"
and *ccrowdded in the
mummirrrorr*

olvido

,roof ,towel ,loot ,p
ill palaver ,the ra
tes of storm be tides
ah uh fflog the g
ate counted paw ,sp
oon ,peel ,run a run
..."simple" .)flapping i
nna chain link f((ence
sent sorta ,dog lay
ered with a ,boot
crumbl ing in its
dirtt))dug ugly
,ham(,knot ,seem
,stood in line at the
bburning bbank

olvido

root flaws ,seen the
rustic es ,pend ant he
el que o primía in
conciente loaf of br
read the)inkspit(
so aked into the mu
d d u mm yr)u
seless con densation(
rattlledd losst on d
own the rroad
the)))sttorm guttt
ers(((in my d
)im ssoaked(ffeet
you ,sleepping on a b
bench box of snn
akes drying in the

basemmmentt

olvido

real dribbbly was nor
meal said a sllummbe
red cru.mb was ,r
awly ,twitted ,"aimed"
ah ettched into is p
ocket ffray ed w
as hhigh clloud wwind
~ ~ ~ rolling *clown* the
,meet yr ,bblank
shudddered]mind[h
a)thru(*the uh door*
"knew the food and
knew the page and
knew the wrinkling
of his cronoshirt h
is" **shoe** *fraught wit*
h eyyes

olvido

toot luck ,Rinse ,so
ot ,sock ,tore the
,rootmaster lunchy in
my throat my ,last top
yawn ,beast ,loomer ,lur
ks ,never missed nor ,p
lot fog ,luster net em
drinko loom ,born to
,sky shout ,tree the
,borers spitting ,the
lunchers growled my
day shutter fire
bloomed an heavy l
ike ,was plunder
,stinking in my
,windy fist

olvido

olvidéme y te olvi
daste olvidente o
lo vivido shot with
fog a gun town
spotfree incor
dado y mis recor
tes se ahogan
ay hoguera hus
shed my backsight
site of shallows
shimmered in my
laundry oliente
ol re lajo vi lo
cuerdo sin impacto
ni intacto oranges
moulding on the fl
oor crowd c
lawing o lo olivivo
foggy like the tum
blur *crawling from
my eyes*

olvido

feet inside the headache opt
to raids the spinning cent
ipede I c lawed the s lap
of c llock gghost ll int dan
cing in the fflashlight k
notty moon ggruñting in yr
pants the ssock sswammp
-----dates the warm lad
der----- got twisst in
textine walked an d
ragged mindd grain sackk
))fishy u((nit w atcch
sllope your f istic
slleeep across the halll the
idle)))tappping of your me
mory air *mundo y murmullente*

olvido

the crawling cream ev
actuation nest the s
wirling bowl your
shirred cloud sacktion
divvies up dawdles
down denser sid
eways peripherectic
chopoff when the cei
ling falls your cup
with plaster fills o
hissing in the ears be
fore the handle sh
ake !

))*ni lago ni cloaca*((

olvido

loss words con
densed the hor
izon mirror "me
ans" ear nothing
mind jaw mask in
the girdle city e
ra sed leaf silence
somewhere in the
river dust til
ted bottom we
dding sludge mot
or dancing in the
c rumpled sweat s
ubu rbs moo
n stat ue g
reen lak e))skull((

Swallowing Ivan Argüelles'
"words" & "at the oriental institute"

olvido

cooler lice suit *such wind*
toil razor cloud your lucky
shirt whistle and a grinding in
the laundry where the ,aim
for floor yr gummy piss I
filled the cuffs)*dog lint*
folder(crust and crust c
rust the top wander
did I shave the yogurt
off ?)in your rage f
arting ,paper bags(*the*
ton twister snaking on
yr rain horizon

olvido

sneezefield what my doggy
blouse blew to revelation
fraught with horns and
fantods banged against the
fence my)sleeping pool(my
))stinking rock((my)))ash
tunnel(((walking toward your
door a single arf a))))shoe((((
)))))peeled bees(((((buttons
named with blood your))))))w
ristless hair(((((((a book sm
oulders in yr hat but wh
at spattered saw was born
was died was transformation
in the black oiled weeds

olvido

shoulder water an my wave *re*
petition the soggy blade my
leg remeats my *repe*
tition where my your po
cket cheese finds the *rep*
etition scrawls the nu
mber same the numb *r*
epetition ur swallow off
the elbow juice *repetit*
ion nods all closet
treasure *repetition* dust an
gritty sock *repetitio*
n ease yr fading b
ones yr *repetiti*
on itching like a g
nat repeats *repeated*
in yr r ear no wonder
they call you King of the World

for Blaster *"All Different All the Same"*
Al Ackerman, who added the last nine words

olvido

..sot...lint....flame..... pees
towel the))lake((craw
miles into the throat a
]soap[ )))mud(((a licor
lit crowding the rakes
your where sheet or mus
cle rises toward the g
))))room((((relents an
wins ,shards ccruncching
in the....gravel....*la botella
el olvido el lúmen la ca
calavera* my sodden
)))))neck(((((*"bravely
filled"*

olvido

should shudder nap lens
coughing in my left lung the
lung left hillock clung
with lint and crawdads
where your tepid lake
crowded on my flabrication
froze it with an alphabet
of flies your whirring
tooth sizzles where my
tongue ought to be should
shoulder flat toss
the mayo off its shiny
turkey slice a sloshing
in the right pills and
dung folded in my
watered blanket where
your gnatty window snores

olvido

tod topo tuerca "the
dick bomber")loot lake
dot(spread my belly in
the))mud((twin tongue
gorged Ah my *and* hat
luncheon fogged with tu
mor the)))twisting rind(((
the tape the black))))cloud((((
drifts into my shoe your
soap floating ,was ,in my
)))))ssoouupp(((((

olvido del fever direction

fever segment what lingered what
shouted future regimes lengua
tronada exhaus if it nt c
rashed the wall interventionis
t hair sink media luna
source material drowning s
pace the poetry scale se
abren los lápices transcriptic
isoclam tolerance takking
plunge fork's teeth and
anguage silt dysfuntional
burning in the O grey
skin visual visociety a
bout the dog clock footpaths
yelmo que "entiendo" book-
plank panic uhuh pork-
loss concrete cenote de
libros drools the true
jején a solas pregnancy
spinning the necrosis glass
spring snake palab rotas
rhetorix sed conejos clus
tered hubbewtee shot
mouth wall dream street
socks casket extrópico
wax ads doghair clot
mir rored night events
stereo nooztotl the whi
mpered chains screen
typing gnats swallowed

in tlapalli in tlilli bir
thpla no presente that
extra bee los lentes y
el centro boats trans
formed una muñeca
enumeronte expands
class bomb pared par
tida flat revolution la
más cara re versal smoke
toward central drain my
vacuum manual tongue I
thought innate libraries
fog cuadrada var ior
existences revoisal center
questions with mud
might delving buttocks
seismic rotting bees
spinning bowl eros corn
a cloud if insular
thigh gatherings ersatz
leak oscillates effluenza
duties of the putrifact

horizontal signs in all directions

Found in Jim Leftwich's
Six Months Aint No Sentence, Book 21, 2012 and
John M. Bennett's *Liber X*, Luna Bisonte Prods, 2012

olvido

the glued tooth ¿washed the
floor ...clods of crowds sc
uttle along the baseboard ,l
intcloud ,*"rainy pen"* the w
atch to the wall nailed ,n
ever chchanged the cor the c
rust occcasion where my
)*ass occcludes*(the foggged d
oor fills my ears)*your win
d*(bawling in the saus
age ay my dentition vis
cous my rigid tongue !
---*found the lost last dime* ◐

olvido

really snored an boiled en
la cumbre ,cobre ,si co
bre ak era y sangre no
,en la toalla me son
aba ,cleaned the w
all clamored like a
metal sleep a leaf I
*ww*ishshed you were
,un cocido una cuca
racha por el sueño
médico *an injection*
I was drank)the
needle apneotic in
the mattress_____(

olvido

the "awful wind" the tied
lap rejecta squirreling on
the floor my brimming s
hoes if air impulsed if
not a snore a crowder
loud a boom nor whizzle
where the page's tore my
pants repatterned in
the blow the back an
choke the rice ro
tting in your shoe k
notted rigging swi
rrllling like yr laun
dry like yr swwolled
hairs yankking yr
coined eyes *off into the mud*

olvido

each lolling rats the plug
towel meats the madder
fork connoiter where the
sissors fog or waits
the each boiling gnat o
bomber flame nut piled
the walls and legs in
to the street !the
calling the bats the
lathered glass ,names
and ,"mild" guts
dancing where the se
wer blew and all the
laundry drifts off
east *my shoes with*
bees filled))*if bees*

olvido

*un olvido de lunch last lint my
loop ,mud neck olvidadizo el
timbre la tumba el trueno mis
olvidos de Manuel Acuña ol
vidado en una plaza polvorosa
con arañas y páginas my
gaseous leg shining in the
garlic patch mis olvidos
del open sewer beside a
field a fish snapping in
the air above un olvido
carcomido e íntegro olvidos
entornados los ojos inol
vidados me he olvidado el
olvido huehueteótlico mis
olividos abiertos en la
ventana abierta en la
muralla de los vientos*

olvido

I forgot my speech re
membered forgot the for
k rusting in the sidewalk
un olvido del concreto des
trozado forgot mis olvidos
supurantes submergidos en
el superficie remembered
forgetting mis olvidos o
valados ovipartos ni
obvios ni oníricos mis
olvidos avalados vigas
del lado izquierdo de mi
cráneo olvidados en el
derecho donde el lago
licuefaciente de mis ol
vidos se me acuerda
y veo *el aire del maíz*
transparente

olvido

foam the clocker lint co
llapse the fly mus
cle draining]]gate[[
louder than ,wristless
buzz where the ticking
lanyard's strangling in
my T-sshirt ssweaty
like a ssteak a ssl
umber ssausaged in
the luminescence ssw
irling in your bathtub
where the songtines
forking in my veins
a lumpy one a
bloody rake

olvido

,dust ,rice ,comb ,wh
eel twisting in the road
my bile nod the bl
inking raft off my
laundered face a cr
ust singing in the
hills the rotting fog
the rubber shoes the
drunk knot I s
lept in Santiago de
Chuco más de cien
años with the corn
the cross the pen po
inti ng down the
sierra toward un
tombeau *une pierre*
blanche une pierre
noire

olvido

de nibbana the pronouns
vault in the dictionary of
anabasis slogging through
salt and Pedernales
small leaves bloodless
pirámide waves in the
underworld driverless in
Vera Cruz Buddham dome
skeleton of erebos off
and on the enigma
of lunar smoke and
murder water

in the end rag ,blisters
,fishes recording ellipses the
,error burnt

Dozing in Ivan Argüelles'
"(anabasis)" & "(nibbana)"

olvido

dot sore mode my sh
irtless flueting save the
lung for sandwich and a
sleep)))washing in the
"murder water"(((brui
sed c l o u d s dr
ooping ,shaved my arm my
contfusion viscous in
my hat my dor mer of
dusty wasps and brittle
ants legs in air the
fallen corners punto
final y mis lagbios es
cupen el titubeo de tu
pena de tu "alba fingida"
smeared across the wall

olvido

mis chewings mis trancas m
is tornillos salpicados en mi
chin mis chispas mentonadas con
una frase de moco mestizo mez
colanza del jamón del aire de
un *"ayer inmiscible"* slogging

through uh **C**ave of tissue
and bats ,rain and bowls of
ice .tantra monta ,mi

sueño)*olvidadizo*(mis c**U**m
bres motilantes motinantes en
contradas por un callejón *con
salida* y mis zapatos los
echo por el río *el río
que sube cuesta arriba*

olvido

the ssorted sshadow chimess a
cor nur mured where my lap
ssed th ought'ss a crissc
raw))*meaty foot mile*((ah
dang led russt ling in the d
rain my ssee med t haw
a ss pelt leaf de lettered
ssp ring deletreadoss loss g
ritoss in son deadoss la ssom
bra del ssissmo]]*ful
minante*[["sslept beneath the

dusst" the **t**owerr ssplit the
tongue *lathered toward the f
inal para graph*)sseeping
ssailing ,sstinging greasse(
was the wind a fork ?

olvido

rule's the rain last month's the
flying field the splintered le
af scis sored ,tousled *on the
trembled fence* yr s
kin fissure ,t h e r e ,a fla
pping for the dessicated c
loud whistled g ate s
peed history *that never*
,comb yr lung com puesto
es ,*con la luz mortecina*
o "tocino" ,)chispas ,*fuentes*(
secantes in the sol ol
vidado no hay tuna no hay
,murmured shale sli pping

from the cli*ff* yr lengua
restiva ,resting ,*restless
in yr shirt*

olvido

on the stunned *l*adder where the
bees brained the boiling grass
the mouthed garage my
spatial step a cube formed
lodged against my spine a
long snore issue dripping in
the guttered pages like a
door your foot bleeds in in
.the verso ,if voiced ,a recto
was ,wrecked between
the ,if papery ,white
,thighs ,down the upway
rests each rung ,when
stepped not ,told and
tolled .*two clouds, a*
bove the tree ,join a far

olvido

*change the fog slather ch
ange the bomb fork the
solid whistle change the
coughing soup monster
washed against your leg
what change the lacker
stool fumed the st
inking bowl wallets cha
nge the coarse swallow
what was seeping in
your lap the brush of
gnats sweeping outward
sudden wind empties
spoon you changed
your hand I scuttled
for the warm schmutz
behind the fridge my
change scalding in my
pocket when the win
dow shattered in my
changer slicing through my
hat my changeless skull's
fumes swirling in the
kitchen timer*

olvido

loop the thrown ball nap
kin changer sank ,or
blank nostril changed
the ,ester folded ,bo
OM mist meat .the too
l the t ool ,with knuck
le fraught ,crashes
down the steps my
brimming neck my g
ate nestle ,reigned
,itchy from the steel
wool's rusty lint
:*O just inhale your*
inverse cloud s
calded with a n
amed word !

olvido

the denser danse flakey
suit buried with the
turkey bones your fog
scandal rested ,restless
.the mail the nostril the
rutabaga swims in piss
.O bailar infomentados los
pasos informáticos sud
oríficos en el encuentro
perdidos ... mucilage o
motiphage I's **ga**g **g**
in**g** turned and ch
urned away the hole
not so deep but s
leeped enough to
end my hopping

olvido ,drink

name innards tossed the
book torn from streams'
corpses unwinding frost text's
mown wind ,"meaningless"
silk ,riddled mind ah ,groping
abcess in the footpath's center
drawers ,"jackdaw and spinet"
revives sleep's peak radiance
folded in erasure ,pools
,marginless ,mirror bush
,break inside the glove
,lacunae ,eye ,*convex foam*

)*shaded briefly in the transit phase*(

In the leaves of Ivan Argüelles'
"(ago)" & "(antiphone)"

olvido

*L*uz *L*ost *L*eg my corny dung
wallowed mouth toward s ling
,c age h oof ,mil es of g
athering tire floors \\ my mus
cled left eye my sleeping right
// the colonphage the \\ sev
ered meat s even wetter than
the s torm c raw st umping tow
ard the dessicated kitchen where
// my garlic sweats beneath your
shirt \\ *leaning past the broken
fridge* // plunder ,washing ,page
gristle spat out \\ *she darks*
,finds your shoe ,a //toilet
stuffed with thigh

olvido

my musc led b linker wow a
whirring in the ,mount war
,paw s to ,melt an moult
,saw the whopper in a lake
,the grease surf the eyes or
flotsam my ,crowded clod
brake the single gristle was
,plunder an powder my ,ticktick
,swerves ,dives ,lobs a c
racker toward the con ,frontat
ion of your liquid lipids scat
tered con densation I ,}}slept
behind the door that o o
pened once last year
п.

olvido

fffffamefff ff ffforff
o*ffff fffffflagfff*
foggffff ffistffff
*ffsafffeffff fff f*ak
e *ffffusionfffff*
feel*ffff fofcusfff*
fffireffff ffameff
ffffffffuelfutileffff
ffformffanffffff
ffigureffprefferenceffff
foamffffoundfffailsff
ffffffffenderffffff
lutter*fff f fff ff*
fffleeffffleaffff
f footfffoundationff
f f ff fff f ffff fffffffff
fill*f f f f f f f*

olvido

gthe grusted gneck ggut gg
gg runt gggetsg g gggoalg
ggroggggg gcombingggggg g
ggreatg g gggasggggg gglock g
rowlgg ggggluegg g g rit gg
gun g host)gagg(gg getg ggg
gggggloomggg go gg g gazegg g
ggemg ggg gguessgg gggg
gg ggung gglass ggsegggreggg
gategg ggummyggggg gg ggg
ggrowthgggg g ggloveggg ggu
lletgg gg g ggggg gush'sgg g g
gggruel gg g g g   g   g   g   g

olvido

see*e*pt ch*e*ew nodt *eee*ends
clatt*ee*er shap*e*es wall*ee*et w
ind l*eeeee*ess cub*eee*ed th
an *ee*engin*ee*ee k*nn*otty s
lope *nn*umbers i*nnn* my g*nnnnn*ats
coruscati*nnnn*g i*nnn* yr *nnnnn*umber
lambiscatio*nnn*)sal(ivatio*nnn* li*nnnn*k
i*nnn*sta*nnnn*ce coughi*nnn*g coug
hi*nnnnnnn*g *nn*or *nnnn*amed the
*nnn*origi*nnnnn* of yr *ddd*oor *ddd*
*dddddddd*rum ,the *ddd*ock *dd*
*ddd*ate the *ddddd*ot*ddddd* d
one *ddd*imly *ddddd*rainage o
*ddd*day *ddd*oggerel shape*ddd*
*dd*ope*ee*d a*nnnnddd eeenn*n
*ddd*orphin*eee eeennn*nt
ropic *ddddddddddddddddddddd*ust

olvido

*ffff*ace the *fffff*latter *ff*
*ffff*uel *fff*istulithic so*fffff*
tware or yr *ffffffff*ocus *fff*
*fffff*ingered *ffff*lag *fffff*
*ff*ire a*ffff*ter *ff*umes a*fff*t
er *fffff*looown nooooostril
poooooours int*ooooo* the b*ooooo*
ook *oooooo*mphal*ooooo*s l*ooo*
*oooo*se *oooo*j*ooooo* se te *ooooo*l
vida la b*oooo*ca ens*oooo*mb
rada *ooooo* *ggggg*asolina y
tu *ggggggg*asa eng*ggg*omada
se me pe*ggggggggg*a la cara es
mi *ggg*rasa y *ggggg*olondrina
letrada *fffff*looooo*ded an *gg*
ggggggggggggggggggggggggggggg one

olvido

hole in the tempo shirt
shirt shirt shirt sheet
emit word risk pause
and crisp el lamuyo
linguistic fish mile snore
pulmón cluster occluded
soot stux carmesí shut
lake basement plunges
next the blanket meatrug
coil span of ears the
darkest ladder state
textual glass forma for
ma forma forma forma
anarchistic signatures fuego
fuego fuego behind the
circled mask chronological
intransigence beehive foaming
the foggy throat it it it
it it it it it futures
deploying history sphere
errors los pasos in
minentes my slump cast
rubble exchanges muffler
bones the flock of
finance crabs the pork
pandemic nostalgia d
riven languages have
passed the clawed cave
tongue liberates thinking
slivers in the glue rea
son fucking cut-up em
bolismo it's a comicbook

excavada el aire economy
hopping sewn johnee fes
tive blubber self or
desire popoca popoca
popoca varecou rece
beebeebeebeebee
fraug nozzles warehouse
my bum puddle gar
gled stem eftwing be
haviour synthesis rain and
corn masks the lawnmower's
seeping maskks in the
basement lubate hamster
spans forgetting fire un
derground fire worms
milk jacked lúmenes
shat in shadow bífida
staircase chain's role
across yr face audio
monuments the finger blodt
grunt theater's wars corn
flakes breaded plants the
focused dog of lake
suits surgery freedom
mute mute mute mute
intolerable cigars sink
uh plunging leaf uh
paper coal silence
in the sun

Found in Jim Leftwich's *Six Months Aint No Sentence*, Book 22, 2012 & John M. Bennett's *BLOCK*, Book 22, Luna Bisonte Prods, 2012

olvido

*ffff*onoilógico y di*fff*undidos
mis *fffff*ósiles ex*ffff*enestrados y
*fff*estered *ffff*lomax e*fff*
*ff*ective como *ff*intaxis *fff*lu
vial ,*fffff*lu-like ,*fff*ast
er *lllll*amination of the f*lll*o
od yr *llll*ung il*llll*uminado ,*lll*a
bora*lllll* ,*lllll*ánguido ,*lll*omismo
*lllllll*unched my ,a*lll*most fl*lll*ayed
my *lll*exic *lllll*abio o *lll*lava t
r*aaa*ced the r*aaa*ty l*aaaaa*ke
.yr á*áá*mbito inef*aaaaaaa*ble ,*aa*
*aa*shes *aaa*nd s*aaaaaa*gging i
ce yr *aa*ction *aaa*actor p*aaa*id
the *aa*cid cloud the *aaa*ir sh*aaaa*de
*ggg*rowing*ggg* *gg*rit yr teeths
.the *ggg*rounded *ggggg*rab the *ggg*reet
an fork fo*ggggggg* the *ggg*um speaks
yr lip *ggg*rub .*ggg*grab ,sting*ggg* ,the
so*gggggg*y *ggg*un *gg*azes at the li*ggg*ght

olvido

ssseessss the asssh nesst the
grissssstle forksss why masster
lisssster sshavesss the lipssssss
ttorn tttowel ttthudding tttower
whatt I tttttold tthe shortttter
clottttt)gristttle lastt(benttt
eeveeery eeentranceee shadeeed
wheeeen my stareeee my Johnee
eee glazeee eeeyeeee sleeeeept
where the flaaame flaaaagger wept *aa*
*aa*nd *aaa*ired the cha*aaa*ined *aa*
*aaaa*artichoke *aaa* w*aaaaaa*ve
of *mmm*ots *mmmm*ute *mmmmm*
*mm*orts swi*mmmmm*ing in yr n
a*mmm*e the *mmmm*isty s*mm*ile

sssentttt theee aaammmmunition and

olvido

*dddd*destruir la f*eee*cha *dddoo*oon
*dddd*e*eee* *ee*l pájar*ooo*o *ee*n
su caí*dddddd*da *ee*nf*ooo*cad*d*a
¡ay mi *ddeeddoo* in*eee*fabl*ee*!)l*eee*aking
in my sh*ooo*oe yr *dddoooo*gg*eee*dd mi
st))squirms((el *ddd*ía f*oo*rmátic*ooo* f
*óóó*rmic*oo* *ddd*oon *dd*e las h*ooo*rmigas *ee*
eee ín*dddd*d*icee*es *ee*n tu cara cal*eee*
n*dddd*árica c*oo*n*ooo*cid*ddd*a p*ooo*or tu
pulg*aaa* pulg*aaaa*rítica m*ee* cont*ééé* y
t*ee* c*oo*ntast*eee* invisibl*ee* inn*ee*er
r*ee*spiration hacia la s*oooooo*mbra
*dd*e*e*l an*ooo* *ddd*e*e*l añ*oooo* v*ooo*
la*dddddd*ooo *o   o   o   o   o   o   o*

olvido

trrrees and t*rrrr*èss mo*rr*t o im
mo*rrr*tel y*rrr giiigg*li*iing*
fount*aaaaai*in pen y*rr rrrr*ope
sssswa*aaa*atter*rrrr sssi*ing*iiing
sss*la*aaa*pt aagaaaiiii*nst *rraaa*w
w*aaa*all m*iii c*aarrr*aaa*a *rr*u
ti*iila*aa*ante y tu c*aa*lz*aaa*do
i*iiintessstiiiii*naal .me c*a*ant
*a*an me n*aa*ad*a*an me ahog*aaaa*a
n en el *aaiiirrrre rrriiiverrrrrr*
*ii*ino l*aa c*aa*ala*averr*r*raaaa*a donde
te me escondes la *rr*iis*saa* l*aaa*s
flor*rr*ess*ss* en l*aaa* tumb*aaa*a
*iiiii*in*fiiiiiiiiiiniiiiita*aa*sssssssssssss* s s

olvido

*aa*imed the *aaa*sh l*aaa*adder
night h*aa*lf r*aaaaaa*n st*aaaa*red
the eye's dre*aaa*med whe*aa*t
you)cr*aaaaaa*wled(p*aaaa*st
the bre*aaaaaa*thing fridge *aaaa*
n*ttt*s dropping from *t*the ligh*tttttt*
fix*tt*ture yr foo*tttt*prin*tttt*s
*tttttt*wi*ttt*ching on the s*ttt*
ained *ttt*tiles yr s*ttt*u*tttt*ered
air far*ttt tt*hroa*ttt tt*he *ttttt*a
b*lll*e swe*lllll*s yr p*ll*unging
f*lll*lood ah yr facia*lll lllll*int
*lll*aundered ,fe*lll* away ,f*lllll*o
ats beside my *llll*unch your f*lll*ag
my *lll*opside *lllllll*ingua *llll*o*lllll*s
*ll*oose*lll*y in *in aa*t*ll*

olvido

the *www*et hell *iiiinnnddddiii*ca*tii*o*nnn*
*ww*here yr a*iiiii*r sha*dddd*o*www* r
*iiddd*es the throat*www*ay pulse*ddd*
*wwwiiii*th soups *wwiii*th to*nnn*gue
gr*iii*stle an yr *nnn*neck *www*heel ,*sww*
wallo*ww*s *wwiinnd*d a*nn* cro*ww*dd*d*s
.the r*iii*ver sh*iiiinnn*gle ,breast a*nnn*
fl*iiiiiii*ies ,a coff*iiinnn* s*ww*ells
."ouch" ,plu*nnn*d*d*er ,mea*nn*t .the rat
sc*ii*ssors sh*iiiiinnn*e o*nnn* scree*nnnn*

yr *ttt*o*nn*gue eye cut   **off**
)"t*iiii*ime" to(sleep beh*iinnnddd*d
the *dddddddddddd*umpster . . .   .   .

olvido

peelt *mm*onk*ee*y no*rr mm*y fla*mm*ee
*rr*eeta*rr*dant sat been*ee*ath th*ee*
cloud *bbubbbb*ling ,in th*ee eemmbbeerr*
wh*ee*rr*ee* th*ee* d*ee*sk whal*ee* sleept
fing*ee*rr*ee*d in th*ee* phon*ee* y*rr*
stutt*ee*rr doz*ee* y*rr* d*rr*owning
eeyee at 3 o'clock ay scald*ee*d
sho*ee* "*mm*y" wind*ee*d ai*rr rr*ee*mmbb*
*ee*rr*ee*d o olvido olvidado !*mm*y
wall*ee*t my wav*ee mm*y dusty
hang*ee*rr lost b*ee*hind y*rr* f
u*rr*nac*ee* with th*ee* skin th*ee*
*ee*a*rr*s the *rr*ustling at th*ee*
botto*mm* of yr stai*rr*s

olvido

sskiinned tthe ssuuiitt youu wore all
niightt tthe ssttiinkiing corn r
ottttiing iin my closett where tthatt
box of guun breatth tthiinkss
beneatth yr ssock collecttiion
iitt'ss tthe driizzliing of tthe
moon yr wett chiin floods
my coatt II wass ssttarttled
att tthe iindex biifuurcattiion
where tthe ssauussage sspliitt
the güüevoss perdiidoss lass ss
ábanass carmessíiess iin k
nottss youur fork flaglessss
wiindow niighttlessss and
yr frac ssaggiing on
tthe ssttaiirway down

olvido

*fffff*lung the stung *fff*lame lamp
a*ffff*ter shoe I *ffffff*aced the
ffuunngguuss shore the wall *fffff*
lute my l*uuuu*ng po*uuu*red into
the l*uuuuu*ggage where my *uuuuuuur*
nnn's broke)k*nnnn*ots a*nnn*(skin*nn*
my door ig*nnnn*ored yr ,*nnn*oose
,*nnnnnn*ostril ,e*nnn*tra*nnnnnn*ce to
the *ggg*ummy throat fo*ggggg* hig*g*h
*gggggg*ristle *ggg*rowls in my s
leeve the snoring*gggggg* *ggg*gate's
*uuuu*tter)fu*uuu*rnace(fog ,f
ire ,pl*uuuu*nder foc*uuuuu*sed ,on
yo*uuu*r sleeping p*uuuuu*tz *uuu*h
)sssausss*s*age sswallowed ,wasssss
ssssssky wasss osssscillation ssh
aped "*sss*shallow wass ,yr sssocksssss s"

    in the weeds ,a foot   **L**

olvido

bloootteeed in my sssleeeeeep yooou meee
pooormeeenooormeeeadooo ha ,fu
sssiladooo inooombradooo ooo meee
pussseee la gooorra nooo peeensssada
,eessoo pueeesss I flaggeeed ni
mooodooo ,waiteeed fooor theee
chain whistleee)¡a cooomeeer!(
pulgasss ,gargánticasss ,mar s
ooondeeeadooo y misss sssueeeñ
ooosss milpaaasss sssooon ,eeen
sssoooñadooosss ni ,ooolivadooosss oool
vidadooosss theee oooval wheee
eeel ooof my eeeveeery eeeateeen
leeeg ,))mi assspiracióóón tumbanteee

"sssooousss la pluieee,
un oooissseeeau deee ceeendreeesss" – J. Benet

olvido

pawed *mmmy ffoorrmm* but le*fff*t
P*rr*ootheseus giggling in *mmy c*oo*rr*
n*fff*lakes y*rrr*)*ffff*ist suga*rrrr*(
cle*fff*t *mmmy c*oo*nt*ent in the
Cave)*rrrr*rain an *fffff*inge*rr*red
cl*ooooo*uds(the wind*oo*ow trapez*oo*
id *fffff*il*mmm*ed with webby dust
an blu*rrrrrr* I ate a b*ooo*ok stung
beneath the t*ooo*th a)*mmmmm*u*fff*
*ff*led st*ooorrrmmmm*(the
*ooo*wl with w*ooooo*den wing jag
uar c*ooo*n plu*mmm*as de nyl*oo*n y
y*ooo*o *mmm*me *fffff*u*mmmm*é la *mm*
*mmm*az*ooo*o*rrr*ca an*ooo*checida
en la b*ooo*capue*rrr*ta el agua pe*rrr*día
,y sec*ooo mmm*e ani*mmmmm*é a su
*mmmmmmm***i***rrrrrr* r r   r   r   r   r

...so my leg in the mirror...drinks...   – T. L. Aloc

olvido

*shhaapee slobbeerr norr yrr frr
uitteed mind ,bbrreeaatthh of
windows ,inflaattion spaatt
eerreed witthh yrr ttunaa
fishh saalaad)aacid pourreed
on tthhee bbonees(my forrmaatt
ion f a a d e e s intto
aa morrning's mistty streeeett f
leeckeed witth ttrraashh aand
inseectts disttaantt bbooming
ttonguee bbleeeeding on my shirrtt
tthhee doubblee caarraa forrks
intto tthhee meedicinee caabb
ineett whheerree yrr shhoee
sleeeeps ,eescupittaado ,inco
mido ,sus llaamaas viaajaanttees
aaguaa son ,saalivaa deel aairree
futilistta*

...nor, was ashing, cloacas... –P. Ulmón

olvido

sshell w*aa*ss ccoughing bloc*ckk*

ssaacckk b**i**ss**t**urí invissible
,fonología ccaasstaa y vaaccíaa
m*aa*ss putrid ssocckk door
*a*ate my *aa*im in firess ,fog
g*a*atess ,lipss or ,ccraacckk
ling m*aa*zess – bre*aa*th of
ssigl*aa*s ,tumis russting in
the j*a*arss crusshed in ho
less))river cr*aa*sshing down
the mount*aa*in~((~ ~ the
*aa*ge of livered l*aa*kkess
my tongueelessss esstu*aa*ry
where I *aa*te the pl*aa*te of

...be*aa*nss...))))))))**S**sky ,rudder
,phone

...y tragó el comprimido – C. E. Rote

olvido

bes*tt tt*hu***nn***der o ***nn****aii*ll ***nn***eck

*lla*nn*gostta* squ*iirmii*nn*g iinn tt*he
*lliinn*t*t* your cash regress*iio*nn *tt*i*i*dy
boca de or*ii*nna y *lla nn*ube *nn*egra como
mo*nn*tt*añ*ña de agua *ll* s*ll*ep*tt iinn*
a *ttiinn*y rowboa*tt* cou*nntt*ed my
s*iinn*gle *tt*hroa*tt ttwi*ice cou*nntt*ed
)where *ll ll*ef*tt* my wh*iist*t*ll*e ,*llii*
ke a d*ii*ck(fo*ll*ded ,shoed
,worms sw*iimmii*nn*g* pas*tt tt*he
*tt*ongue *ll nn*amed my droo*l*
freddy ,barked before *tt*he *lla*u*nn*
dry hamper where *ll ll*ef*tt* my
arms my ha*nn*ker*iinn*g my
"*tt*o*ii*l*l*e*tt*r*ii*es c*llii*mb *tt*he s*tt*
a*ii*rs *aa*nnd g*ii*gg*ll*e"

...*en el aire, piedras. – H. Or. Migas*

olvido

the bll**a s**ter foork doog *cclloouudd*

what en barking *lluu*nche*oo*n
emp*lloo*dd*e*dd thr*oouu*gh the win
dd*oo*w)"**cc**rap an **icceccuu**bes"(
what I ate reverse*dd* ,*cc*ll*oo*cc*k*edd
yr *ll*eg ,min*dd* an finger ,t*oo*
my *ll*ips the *cc*ll*oo*t raise*dd* ,*ll*
*ooo*ot an praise the *ll*ar*dd* yr
p*oo*cc*k*et b*oo*tt*ll*e*dd* with it)m
y *dd*reaming fang(yr sh*oo*re
,m*oo*t*oo*re*dd* ,washe*dd* the *ll*ake
*oo*ff ,the b*oo*illing t*oo*mb .*oo*h
nest ,*dd*rip my w*oo*r*dd* fr*oo*m

me ,exp*ll***OO***dd*e that b*uu*rger
in my ba*cc*ksi*dd*e where the
*cc*hairs *cc*oo*uu*gh an*dd* fl*oo*at
a w w a y

"...his lunch funneled through a shirt"- I. M. Pacter

olvido

blind washer clo*uu*d *mmy mmuutttteer*eed
*mmuutte tt*hee spoon con*tt*aineed ,yr
divina*tt*ion ,silenc*ee* spok*ee*n ,loo*tt*
r*uumm*bleer nor ,*mmy* ask *tt*een*tt*
)¡whis*tt*lee!(l*úúmm*een nor*tt*eeño

y *uu*na carree*tt*rreera con c**a**beezas c
on pi*ee*s y *mm*anos ,bolsas n*ee*gras
de plás*tt*ico y ví *ee*l pla*tt*o d*ee*
hígados y s*ee*ranos ...o la nada
v*ee*ía ...pré*ést*ta*mm*o deel fin
.*tt*u shi*tt* com*m*ía and yr
bowl *mmy ee*m*m*p*tt*y leeg ree
*tt*uurneed *tt*o a drying p*uu*ddlee

e e l d d *u u* p

a *tt*iny **car** glis*tt*eening in s*uu*n
- a wall of flow*ee*rs - *mm*ee*att*
an *mm*is *t t : : : : : : : :*

"...sa...chaussure, plein de boue" – mr. de Ténir

olvido

I hamm**e**rred lake *t*the *ffrroostt*
*ss*inge*rr* b*rr*eaking in *t*the
*ff*auce*tt* .bi*tt* my *ff*inge*rr*
*ff*a*ss*cina*tt*ioon wa*tt*ched i*tt*ss
bl*ooo*dy nail i*tt*ss *ff*ly in*tt*e*ss*
*tt*ine quive*rr*ed in my b*rr*ea*tt*h
~ ~ ~   *oo* mi*sstt*y ballpeen n

umbe**rr**ed *oo*ne !*t*the b*oo*wl
*oo*ff ca*ss*h ,a ma*tt*ch ,a
*ff*licke*rr*ing wind*oo*w]]*oo*u*tt*
*ss*ide a ne*oo*li*tt*hic *tt*emple
c*rr*umbled in i*tt*ss *sstt*rreaming
hai*rr* ~ ~ ~ ~   I d*rr*ooped
my wa*tt*ch in u*rr*ine ,like
a *ff*lag]]my d*oo*ubled a*rr*m*ss*
a]]l*oo*g bu*rr*ning in a di*ss*

*tt*an*tt*   *fffffffffffffffffffffffffffffffff*oo*rr* **e** *ss*tt

...en la maleta sus calcetines empapados
- M. Erdre

olvido

depende ,dij*oo* .pendej*oo* ff*oo*ccaall
,llaas ccirrus veíaa .p*oo*sitivism*oo*
inffumaante ,s*oo*mbraa ffétidaa
de llaa b*oo*llsaa ffestivaa ell
p*oo*llipr*oo*pillen*oo* negr*oo* de mis

o**O**¡**O**os que ffines de lluz s*oo*n
.embestid*oo* ,ffraagmentaad*oo* ,ff*oo*saa
y ffllaamaante "es" ,e intestin*oo*
e ,intextuaall .dell tech*oo* pende
,reb*oo*llsaad*oo* ,"cc*oo*ncciente en tu
vistaa" y en ell vient*oo* de aayer
,baamb*oo*lleaante .s*óó*ll*oo* llaas
nubes paasaan ,ffirmes y
effimer*oo*s ,ffullguraantes cc*oo*m*oo*

haamburguesaas Ω Ω Ω

her corndog dipped in blood...
-X. Ipe

olvido

*nnot nnom nnor nnumb nnor
nnaatteess nnor minnee ,my
minnd ann innssttaanncee*

onnee ssttaammeer ***f o g***
*nneeighinng inn tthee lightt oo
zinng downn tthee waall* my
ñot my ñom my ñumb ñaattee
sslosshinng inn tthee ttub))¿c
aalleed you whaatt?((haair
aann hottdogss))mileess of
aabaanndonned paannttss yr((
wrissttleess wheeeezee ,cou
nntteed eeveery word waass
"onnee" waass eeveer ...ssh
ouldeereed tthee library dusstt
**,jusstt ttaakee aa sseeaatt aa
tteeaattss aa**

...her ice and fantods gleaming
- E. Ach

olvido

my bea*ttiinng ssttarrtt rrabb*ii*tt*
f*oo*am*iinng iinn* y*oo*urr *nnoossttrriill*
why y*rr* b*oo*w*ll oo*f *ss*hake*ss*
w*iigglless oo*nn *tt*he *tt*
ab*lle* wa*ss* y*rr ttiimiinng*

*ss*h*iirrtt* y*rr* he**aV**ed *ss*h
eett k*nn*oo*tttt*ed u*nn*derr
*tt*he bed *II rr*a*nn iinn*
*ss*i*i*de my face *iinn*
*ss*i*i*de y*rr e*ll*b*oo*w* jumpy
"*lli*ike a c*oo*mmu*nn*ii*sstt*"
my cake sw*iimmiinng iinn*

a bucke*tt* ...Ц))))*tt*he
*nn*umberred fog(((*iiss*oo
*ll*a*ttii*oo*nn*)))*ll*eap*iinng* a*tt*

*tt*he d*ooo*orr ,c*ll*oo*ss*ed   ))) ⊢

Très utile, sa culotte... - St. A. M. Mer

The Olvido of False *Silence*

walk*iinn*g toward th*ee bee*ee who
*iiss*ll*and*ss fa*ccee* rad*ii*o thu*nn*deer
*s*sh*ee*eath*ss* of pla*nn*eet*ss* photo*ss*
formu*llaii*cc pat*ii*o *oonn* th*ee*
pyram*ii*d the *cciitii*ee*ss* ru*t*i*i*ll*a*t*iinn*g
,p*ii*ll*ee*ss a*nn*d lla*th*ee*ss* ,wat*e*er t*ii*sss*s*u*ee*
wh*ee*er*ee* th*ee cciir*ccullar r*ee*ee*d*ss l*ii*sst
eenn iinn your blood or
*ss*e*ee*ed h*ii*sstory humm*iinn*g *iinn*
th*ee* tow*ee*rss ,pap*ee*rbacck
gllass*ss nn*umb*iinn*g *iinn* your
d*ee*n*ss*ee *ss*cchooll

Una caminata por
"(listening)" y "(Mansion)"
de Ivan Argüelles

Olvido de Jeter le Duct Tape

tempora loca qu'un enfant
jette sa baue cigarettes em
bodied pour un poëte aex
thetics apartments de la
scorie social centuries a
rejeté la sienne the salt
of noise un long essor il
tombe memory au jour
mapped horses ni cynique
the copies consume un cilice
ground beef leurs sonnets à
manchettes electromedia
panda et luxes pachaliques
wrapped in centers leurs
buandières blob boom dot
je n'ai jamais tambouriné
catastrophic bare skulls la
bourgeoisie de ma pauvreté
bonetexts platitude de cette
speech meat je donne ce
livre à toi masked riots
métagraboliser le nour
numl infin une populace
fictiotod la lycanthropie le
Missouri ersatz hinterlands
étranglé the bilateral col de
chemise the aubergine the
hotdogs les hommes tués

"...obsclips, ce livre, silver pipe,
tabac de Maryland!" - L. E. Cynge

Found in Jim Leftwich,
Six Months Aint No Sentence, Book 23, 2012
Pétrus Borel, *Préface a Rhapsodies*, 1831.

olvido

eee looseeerr strrookeee across th*eee*
pag*eee* yrr wh*ii*t*eee* v*eee*rrs*eee*
uurriinneee damp a*nn* b
last forrk ,so*uu*rr w*ii*nndow *iinn*

fl*eee*ctii*o*nn of yrr **t**ow*eee*rr*ii*nng
sh*ii*rrt last*ii*mada d*eee*salojada ,pl
*uumíífeee*rra ofi*i*d*ii*osa *uu*nn porr
t*eee*nnto como c*úú*m*uu*lo ,las gotas
q*uu*e*ee* ca*eee*nn *eee*nn *eee*l s*uu*p
*eee*rrm*eee*rrcado t*uu* sanngrr*eee*
*eee*nnvasada pal*eee* vom*ii*t
drry*ii*nng *ii*nn a bowl yo*uu*r *nn*
att*eee*rr*ii*nng sl*eeeee*p t*ii*nny
fac*eee* p*ii*nncheed a*nn* drr*ii*bbl*ii*nng
,booksh*eee*lv*eee*s f*uu*lla d *u u* s t
a*nn* corrnflak*eee*s)))crr*uu*mbl*ii*nng

m o t h   ∂   ∂   ∂

...white verse urine, damp and tiny
- Blaster Al Ackerman

olvido

*tt*ubaal littigaattioonn in *tthhe ffffoog*

yrr *tt*en*tt prroolaapsing* in I cooul
dn'*tt* bre*aa*tthe coould n'*tt ffff*
a*a*ce *tthhe* shhudderring sui*tt*
swi*ffff*tt *tt*aanking in *tthhe
ffff*oorres*tt*'s *tthhrrooaatt aa*y
l*aa*bioo en*rr*ev*esaa*doo *aa*y caalz
oones ***aahhoogaadoos*** en el
*ffff*aangoo)ch*h*oocoolaa*tt*l *aa*uhh
ic*tt*e*tt*l(*ffff*a*a*ke *ffff*a*a*uc
e*tt* emp*tt*ies oo*ffffffff* yrr
"desk" *aa* shhel*ffff tthh*und
erring in *tthhe* woooods *aa*

m*aa*rrble ◐ *ffff*aals *ffffr*room
yrr m*oo*u*tthh aa*)*tt*urd blinker
*ffff*ooaams("*aa*nd *tthhaatt*
swelling ***aatt*** **my neck**"

In tlahcuilolli tlilticmicahuitl...
- Neoc Taotl

olvido

ttuuercaa endemmoniaadaa y en caal
aammbres enttonttaadaa inttonsaa
ffforttaalezaa de mmis ttijeraas
oxidaadaas ttaanttaa risaa ttaa
nttaa ,fffuummigaattion ,fffisttuulaadaa

,ttuummbbaa ttuummbbaa   a
.chaa rred chaammaaco where tthe
hole waas uused tto bbe
tthe "ffforking wraatth" tthe
"issue" ttires)youur stteaamm
ing raatt(ttwistt down in
.corttaar ,corttezaa ,conmmingle
,ttus conejittos cuuttsy spoons

plaasttic d*a*ancing on yr haatt
juustt ttoott juustt bbeaak j
uustt prey aan plaay tthe
effflouurescentt luuggaage d
raaining on yr   b b a a c k

...pesadumbre, tus lentes prístinos...
- C. I. Hego

116

olvido

loo mismoo *ddaaddoo* ,snnaake **e**y**e**s ,*coonn*
ejoo miserrraable the waaves≈ *rrretirrre*
aa✖is munndd*i* the strrraaw foorrrk
cloouddedd with yrrr toonngue
bífiddaa)aaddifíb(*ddooblaarrr laa oonn*
ddaa perrrddiddaa enn loos cinncoo
senntiddoos baack up *aa*n
listenn .)toowels *rrrustinng* i*nn*

the trrrunnk *a*a(syrrup s

leeve *aa* ,crrroowdd bub*b*li*n*ng
oonn the *rrruunnwaay* wherrre
uh zoopiloote ...wennt this
waay thaat ,grrrinnedd inntoo
my *ddoorrrknnoob* boowl grrrinn *aa*
*nnd*d swaalloowedd yoourrr

k   e   y

...y el tormento del agua con arroz.
- P. Aella

olvido

n**a**mme the sshore glandd youur

touussledd ddossïïïmeter whïïïsstless
where yr tonguue quuackss losst

the puusstuulencïïïa fooammïïïng on the

mmuuddss porch tïïïmme nor brïïïckïïïng
where the sshaddow thawss the

blïïïnkïïïng ssuurf not ,passssïïïve
lendder crowdd ,typer buu

riedd ïïïn the ssandd yr dd

ïïïctïïïonary of wïïïpïïïngss ,the
long brown ssmmearss fromm

A to Z andd puunct uuatïïïon

collapssïïïng on mmy lever *III*

wass *III* wass not wass y

ouu ,sspelledd andd ddrïïïbblïïïng

ïïïn a sspell the vacant ss

uurf wïïïth ddrawiiing fromm

t**h**e

Lo famélico, crisol de mi lengua.
- F. Ormatique

olvido

loo**g** c*c*oo*rrnnnn* ,was a s*c*c*at sha*rr*d gliste*nnnninnnn*g foo*rr*m too*oo*l a m*oo*uth *oo*f seeds)y*rr* teeth(

⌐⌐⌐ t*rr*ipled stu*nnnn* y*rr* c*c*oombed c*c*heek ...lau*nnnn*de*rr*ed th*rr*o*o*ugh the wo*oo*ods... y*rr* loost sa*nnnn*d wi*cc*h))*rr*oope f*rr*ied a*rr*oo u*nnnn*d y*rr* *nnnn*egck((the loo*nnnn*g last time)))satu*rr*atio*onnnn* *oo*f the live*rr*(((whe*rr*e the falle*nnnn* c*c*heese the))))mist beloow the *rr*ive*rr* ,eddy *oo*f plasti*cc* bags((((my lapsed t*oorr*tilla slumps be hi*nnnn*d the c*c*oompoost bu*cc*ket)))))chai*nnnn* *oo*f a*nnnn*ts a(((((spide*rr*

da*rr*ts i*nnnn*too a))))))c*c*rra*c***C**k((((((

...pisantes, mes lèvres sourdes s'effacent.
- O. Z. Totl

olvido

uh dri*b*ping ne*g*ck
s)ilent sho(**e**

the went wall

olvido

brush c *raw*

libp **c**u*t*

)the ,rest((((

olvido

shnore ,tuube

).).)...rice lake...(.((

the choking towel

olvido

,beet ,mountain
,lure ,fork
,tide ,intestine
,ham ,lung's
,boil ,

p))lung((,**e**

olvido

ah murder
wrote "Table"

the bell the clout

)**bomb**(er

olvido

cl*a*y an s**n**ort

*fly p***i***le*

pig rocket

...brine ,ba**l***loon*...

olvido

]*effing cheese*[

lake

olvido

moo)d f(use

was p t *orn*

]]*the mind er file*[[

"sap"

olvido

*t*tea*tt* s*tt*roke ,sau*cc*e len*tt*il ,*tt*ub
sugar w*hh*ere my *iitt*c*chh* relapsed
a s*cc*ore node a flying *tt*i*i*me

roos*tt*er s*hh*aped *tthh*e *hh*op mu*t*te//

bus,*t*ter nape yr ,bre**a**s*tt* d
ry*i*ing *ii*n *tthh*e *cc*orn so **a m p l e**
,spre ad*i*ing *ii*nna)) bowl ((
≈]yr s*hh*r oud[≈)))dro,,wned(((ay
me fa*cc*i*i*al ≈la()ke≈ "sees" yr
&kno*tttt*i*i*ng& c.h.o.k.e.s on's s**P**oon
:::::soup fog::::::: broke lo *cc*omb*ii*
na*tt*or*i*io "y en *C*cholula esperaba"

...goa*tt* pa*tthh* of •• s*tt*ones and
■ boxes el *t*teléfono de la es
qu*i*ina sonaba y sonaba la

....neblina circular al fondo de la cuadra....
- S. Ordo

olvido

en el su*rr ll*a *lll*luviaa vi*d*rrioosaa
en e*ll* baambú l*aa tt*errmaall oo
oo**j**oo de *ll*a nieve mis n*oo*ttaas

*aa*llttaazzoorr**i***aa*n*aa*s *aa*y)cumbrre(in
*aa*llc*aa*nzz*aa*ble c*oo*nn bb*aa*anderr*aa*
de niebll*aa* en mi m*aa*llett*aa* y
en mi m*aa*llett*aa* un f*oo*c*oo* el*l*
equip*aa*je e*ll* c*aa*llcettín n*oo*
pe*rr*did*aa* y un libr*roo* c*oo*n
c*rr*ettoo un ⊠ *ll*aad*rr*ill*ll*oo un
anill*ll*o⭕ *oo*xid*aa*d*oo* ,p*aa*sttell de
híg*aa*d*oo* del "su*rr*" en mi m*aa*llett*aa*
ll*aa* f*aa*c tt*u*rr*aa* de *tt*rres c*oo*mid*aa*s
úl*l*ttim*aa*s mi c*aa*mis*aa* escrr
itt*aa* c*oo*n piscoo y *aa*jí c*oo*n
f*oo*tt*oo*s sin *rr*iñoones c*oo*n
*ll*ib*rr*oos lleíd*oo*s *aa*vec *ll*es
yeux fe*rr*més)qué l*aa*tt*aa*
qué ni m*oo*d*oo* decí*aa* qué

...pulga dormida en el itzcuintli.
- Dr. Atl

olvido recte

erect in the invisible page e
rect in the faucet half er
ect in the prefabricated root ere
ct in the anthropology window erec
t in the tilted suit erect
in the fire's flame
erect in the fog or minute e
rect in the grassy eyes er
ect in the naked grammarian ere
ct in the neck's bridge erec
t in the drunken bunny erect
in the unfinished fugue

Sitting up in Ivan Argüelles'
(mountain) & (crossing)

olvido

,r
eeling ,slowing ,shading ,c
locking ,paging ,tombing ,m
aking ,docking ,farting ,c
hanging ,pissing ,phoning ,s
heeting , sleeping ,moulting ,n
aming ,drying , pilling ,b
reaking ,gazing ,gauging ,k
nowing ,mindlessly ,baulking ,p

lunging ,*g* aging ,dressing ,un
dressing ,grimacing ,hugging ,s
creaming ,not toweling ,breaking ,l
addered ,mumbled ,blasted ,th
inking ,crawling ,standing ,k
illing ,facing the luggage p

*a*cked for tomorrow ,s
welling ,roiling and crow
ded *"like a lake full of
hamsters"*

pulgas, libros, ojos...
-D.Or Mido

olvido

meat an mutter the ,aftergrow
sweaty on yr half-worked back the
grunty sun figured in figured out my
slack)*mask*(,crisol imbuído la
,pantomima imbuída ,de lungs and
rabbits ,time to thaw and time
to ,frozen leg glitters in the free
zer))*plunger*(( )))*dot clot*(((mor
ning metal ,blots against the wind
owed sky]]]]*dizzy be*[[[[f
ore the ,breezy slivers time col
,lapsed yr lunk phonetics or
pork rendition sammich some
ding wheeling on the back porch
motaphysics the nest for one
known ,then gone

I am a lunk.
-Blaster Al Ackerman

olvido

t**ï**ny sugar*kkkk* ,high *kkkk*mute speeder note's the fork*kkkk* wheel ,*kkkk*sprayed the single stone*kkkk* notside ,*kkkk*lam ination in the *kkkk*doubted sink*kkkk* *kkkk*mutation where I sank*kkkk* my *kkkk*tongue your foc*kkkk*us on the swirling*kkkk* drain to where my disappear*kkk*ing face*kkkk* reversed its *kkkk*course)yr*kkkk* adolescent diary buried in*kkkk* in smelts( ))corn*kkkk* syrup drying*kkkk* in yr*kkkk* hat(( )))my boiling *kkkk*watch loot(((infusion*kkkk* dribbling*kkkk* off the tines *kkkk*why s*kkkk*weaty neck*kkkk* why))))fing*kkkk*ers ((((

...l'eau abominable de mes doigts.
- M. U. Lulation

olvido

shirt school your dust yo ur
paw ing ah p late st
omach neck um my see
pair uh my .pellet dog
,high *eeeee* noter odd
,dun g ear ,w ailing f
or a s tart ah .pee
l ,shoed ,d rug ,nor m ass
if wa tered dow n the sh
adow ,l earned to p ocket b
reathed the mot es sp
illed the lo x p latter .)b
ut n ever butt oned(
))w rote an he ard ent
e red((teet h tab lets
in my gull et mel ts an
ever y thing)))for gets(((
)))))   ((((

...e as ilhas esquecidas em chamas
-S. O. Dade

olvido

wrote past socking I mute
met severed shaver combed
the tuna salad pocket b laze
cor e s and min d w
hump and ***be es*** yr
b log s hoe yr ,w heels s
leeping in my ,nad a mem
ored in the *heavy shorts* I
drop ped be side the toil
et w here yr see n re
membstruats my ooo)h and
b oiled in the cor n(ooo
))*the halted fur sinks,,,((*
)))ooo"**bubbling shoe**"ooo(((

...lorsque boue, lorsque langue...
- Jean Benítez

olvido

elbow crime *wall* the
torn *deck* my

shattered an slathered
,stuck it in the yogurt

olvido

trots an clouds
the bill
the fist the bowl

olvido

raw ham b
other root drool

*pesa
tanto*

la llanta

olvido

try to
swerve list
pill grime
the *folded* ,one

olvido

crime bill
clouded yakking

the faucet

piles an flames

olvido

tongue ,mort
mild while
you bas
turd

)chew(

olvido

saw savor
where the whelp
muscled

tomb

olvido

shipped and wallowed
bide and dead

) *the wrinkled sky* (

olvido

my rat trunk
un pelo ralo

por
matona

)es encia(

olvido

swelling trawling
buying trailing
mutely))tumbled((

fog wrassled
,blinder today

olvido

Lunk rat my ,seeded shawl sky ,damper ,blood tomb ,race of th umbing f orks hah)head(d ense sleeping on the lentil p late))*yr core cough*((st utters yes olvido of the lunked desk !*mailed* ,bones ,*rabbity an the gristled c* lock suit short steamy wrath n odding in my sweat force *of cheese* ,wheels ,dog teeth .)))*my awful water*(((an the ice contraption clouds))))*peluca se pulca pe loco*((((

...loosely waded in the scrawling dirt.
- P. Ile

olvido

"mutely mattered"
nor
pisant & pleasant

bull heel

∘∘∘≈)*lather!*(≈∘∘∘

olvido

the squirted rug
the white lamp fog

)))*spin spin*(((

olvido

le‍ss than cheese your so

apy flake conniption
,fit for ralph sandwich
and a slugged meat a
ball corner fleeling weak
o shapeless simper ,)*work
at least for me*(,was
more than lip thirst m
ore than towelled sky
))⎯⎯⎯⎯⎯⎯((the brea
king fork)))*soon the
chittering bowl*((( ))))*yr
dog clocked seen*((((
)))))*less than slabbed
ham drink*((((("my c
loudy water dri
pping from your shoe"

...ni agua muerta en el mar atontado.
- C. A. Carío

olvido

ni *ppp*ústula ni grano *ppp*os
terior tus tetas *ppp*len
itudinarias y *ppp*or *ppp*lectro
,*ppp*or so*ppp*a de *ppp*a*ppp*a
y meada *ppp*or no*ppp*ales men
ores y *ppp*ulmón ¡ay sondeo
del la*ppp*sus *ppp*latus ,*ppp*o
rquería diamantina de
tu gorra intestinal !)ni
*ppp*an ni lu*ppp*us la*ppp*bio
mi *ppp*lomo(   )))se*ppp*elio
de las muertas del no
rte sin se*ppp*ulcro es el
*ppp*aso *ppp*alma ,*ppp*
almos y *ppp*ulgas *ppp*
enetrativas y *ppp*erdidas
,itinerario del *ppp*ositivilismo....

...she was coughing what the rain forgot.
- G. A. Bécquer

olvido

my lobster fuel ,deck of
carne de cloaca ,mild
piles semidesnudas ,*tum*
befactos los chéveres pu
ercos grises de la mo
neda ,que clatter in the
tank such drink ,agüita
de cerote ,pulmón ren
dido ,salmón gelatinoso en
el fondo del fridge)))≈*your*
lake≈(((crusted corpses see
ping in the banks burning
clothes on all the aceras
de los hospitales ay mi
facial eating !))))foam
rising in my throat....((((

...manger tes jambes dans l'eau...
- M. Er. l'Elevateur

olvido

esss camote esss ,pill ssshirt esss
,clamor o tunasss podridasss
,sssilla ssshimmering in the sss
ump pump hole yr))))foggy
ssshadow((((sssandwich de un
pessso essspecial para ,lo
misssmo lo inaudito lo pla
sssmático y sssonogramático
en el essscusssado nocturno
- where yr sssweet potato
fell -)))dark with mot
or oil((( ))tendencia sss
weaty((- or the sssugar
- barking ,*ladeado para
no ver nada* - la esss
encia ssshapelesss)an
yr mazorca de sssueño
enfangado(

...the lesser lists were lost in the toilet.
- Dr. G. A. Rabatos

olvido

wra**SS**ling the boiled *t*
ongue su it your shifty linda era
,portent of the clam disection
,disecada ,pulmenórico ,the
knotted arms your fancy
lake ,*piles in yr shorts*
.said ,la lengua fósil ,tru
er shirt or ,muse of sh
ame sure was the toggled
dirt crime ,charred
legs strewn on the bank
.el discurso momio ,los
yelmos de aceite brimming
,"*o sleep in the cups of sea*"

...l'âme médullaire, brindis oubliée.
- V. Omir

olvido

cama flAma ,nekkid soga de
mis lustros lastimados ,mebbe
slippery ,mighta shoot ,fi
gúrate .the mighty sheet
hot *"qua qua"* jerky at
the rope's end ,espejo
misti ,the tidy flake be
fore the fridge genuflection
)*yr claim's shoulder ,sky*(
faster frog gland an my
mountain mastication ,sal
ivalor ,lo fumigado ,un
taco de llanta con su
chile ,sal ,de aquí la
,impensable ,impresuroso
,prisa famélica de mi
calzado canceroso ¡o e
quipaje transluciente
,nunca pensé en tí!

...double, and a tineless fork.
- Luis de Góngora

olvido

*M*imo ,mato ,moro ni acá mi
acullá nor siempre simpered
in the acequia asquerosa de
,un túnel tumbled with
a brick)*nor snore*(cápsula
del aire ,tomb of lemurs
.my face cloud retreats in
side yr manga filled with
wind ~ ~)*shorter bray
the*(sang towel rung a
cross the moat *blank
thud blank thud* ¡ay
swelling of the cogote f
looding of the maze!
))*pesto macho ,sweeping
where the plates con
geal*((

...carcomido, el auto del aire.
- Vicente Huidobro

olvido

*T*asty shadow ,tense of las
t camino under the wall w
here a single turd's shrivel
led corn an diamonds scatte
♩ ♩♩♩♩ ♩♩♩ ♩ ♩♩♩♩♩ ♩ ♩♩
red in the dust el)*lago de
mi nuca*(pico alambrado
,*sabor de páginas y petró
leo* ...*chewed the hand t
hat bed you short of* **R**
and **L** *the ast anguage
g umbled down the iver*...
faced the corner ,cloud
.b utter time ,nor scis
sored cheek "*el riñón
final que cae en el
polvo dicho*"

...et les mains, remplis d'ampoules.
- Dr. B. Lessé

olvido

a*bbbb*sorb*b*ti*ii*on cake *bbbbb*ed my
thro*bbbbbb*ed sorti*ii*ng cha*iii*n lum*iii*n
esence of *bb*baged se*iii*ze cor
n my caroti*ii*d starv*iii*ng yr
su*bbbbbb*terfugue an shorts
)tasted m*iii*nd recal*iii*b*bbb*rati*iii*on(
yr sore *bbb*banana sl*iii*pery *iii*n
the s*iii*ngk *III* woke to *bbbbb*
oom*iii*ing woked to sla*bbb*bed
the lenses off the ∞))stunned
cloud locker((∞ *bbbb*led my
pocket muff*iii*n)))ape cr*iii*
sp(((an yr sh*iii*fted shore
was l*iii*ght that a ,crawi*ii*ng
6 AM the swi*iii*ngi*ii*ng sheet th
e))))*bbbbbb*b*iii*nder of yr ch

alky sk*iii*n (((i*B*

...el ronroneo de tu piel.
- Manuel Acuña

olvido

thhhat moonster hhhamlurchhher ,sw
eat noooose ,hhhung a shhh
apless gate an)fluttered(
a))looaf of eye((gasping
oon the hhhill yoou guttered
oon doown ahhh anent thhhe
,shhhrug moorter ,"soooon"
)))phhhiloosoophhhe(((my gu
mmy nood ...st ink far an
w ide... ...las casas ahhhoo
gadas... leaf redactioon
ay me shhhoorn foooot in
tact isle smooky shhhoo
ver a))))y hhhum thhhe moo
ooning noostril hhhalf oof
diamante hhh alf o'o'((((}my

wandered **k**nee{

...indagar el auto agua...
- Alvar Núñez Cabeza de Vaca

olvido

raw was ,*t*the *tt*tee*tt*h soap ,ins*ttt*
an*ttt* fulminesco *t*the ,lasered face
crawls *t*the ~braid~)smoking
*ttt*omb( ))*your bread dog*((a d
ying *tttt*rain   .eh s*tt*teak f
older ,yr pills a con ,cre*tt*e
shoulder *tt*tired in a)))mirror *t*the
window ahead((( ))))cloudy wi*tt*h
yr hair((((*tt*thunder an
a blink • = "I burbled in my
shoe commencemen*ttt*" you
)))))were esblow*tt*teric on *t*the
fingered sky

...la garganta que comido he.
- César Vallejo

olvido

)("*hot meat*")(surf laundered step
my wavered s tone lap sus))fla
g cave((the withered shape ah
rest !the .*frayed an lock an*
dip sheet a n ,)))peel(((the
gris tle]comb bomb[yr g rime
blistered or]]fork[[ ))))the
steamed be es ,yr *h air* }heat
my wrist{(((((the fog the sh
oe the ,th undered leg ...)(slos
hed up in the blender)(*wh*
ere yr knife drunk in

...*en el viento sanguíneo del aire*...
- Netzahualcoyotl

olvido

the u.gly l.unch .the
belted cro.wn .I .said re
.pile .sweat .nor f
inger ti.me .s.tay a.
.while ga.ming .ovu .la
.tion ate what .bur
.ned .the sky my wh
.eeling p.hone .)pl.a
.ced yr t.rousers on
,my(head b.lister the
sky's ape ,hor.izonte s
.in de.dos o "Cha.n
.cho Div.ino" squ.irming
on))my((p.late

...elbow dung...
-Walt Whitman

olvido

hot meat chain ,the door shoe
welter or the water barking sh
adow where my eye beneath the
surf the other sees a hill of
muddy towns]la diosa paja
rera[what a blutwurst in my
pocket meant the beakers
brimming from yr neck re
lease]]I *slept*[[ ]]]inside yr
drained fog[[[ ]]]]a pud
dle[[[[ ]]]]](())[[[[
in my heat sandal)))flood an
mist :::::: (((

...looser...
-D. Rown

olvido

chewing the sore luncher an my
shirt leg stone the mud
lake wheels drains the craw
ling doors my sticky blood
pooling in a fluted shell your
northern crime log crisol del
mar las cabezas inmentadas
or my stinging lake .arm
drained .la bruma vista el
túnel carnal el picchu por
tátil de mi)corazón o
pie(en el ventilador un
teddy bear sin ojos y
respiro el zapato derecho y
me despierto en el izquierdo

La pornografía es una ventana.
- Iztac C. Alzado.

olvido

sumo dicho la M al me forked
,shiny skittering or)haw suff
erin' succotash(a gate spu
rting like the bean dip last
night's dark eats over a
crumbling phone outside the
garden ~crawls~ *through the
heat* ~ ~ ~   ~   ~   ~   ~

olvido

*olvido scurrilous ,rain town mis
lodos escritos fire scra
mbling in the shirts I
wore a touseled wall mu
ralla impendejada mas
seria ,ni fonética su
rly clawed por el cai
mán temporal the clou
dy thorn the toppled
wheezing of yr gla
ndular fork its sev
ered whistle its
green mask buried with
the sausage skins .my
ground recall my gri
nning vomit in the corner*

"...chingón el libro de hule."
- Manuel Gutiérrez Nájera

olvido

as a basket of beans I
was buried – listed in the
grunting fog the dirt
rains on my pictures]*sh*
eets[my spooned luggage
crowded in the hall]]*con los*
libros transculturados en Mani
en Tezcoco[[the thin god glop
]]]"thinks"[[[mi]]]]*texto*[[[[
leguminoso the sand was
rivered a squamous]]]]]*bifold*[[[
[[ch arred in the dust ,I looks
up from the hole flutter
my cheeks "una lágrima" *co*
mo dijo el fraile flailing ,ojo del
mero mierda

...y frijoles no somos.
- C. Acá de Landa

olvido

h*O*t sheet flood dry)slug
plate(*stool bomber where*
my floated denk slivered in
the cold the))shirt for got((
)))*mist and rugs*(((my face d
rained be neath the be d o
swivelled comb !))))east the
sing shadow ,minded phone ,s
wallowed dust an fork ,ay cro
ssed hairs pulsing in yr
windless breath ~ w hat
humm s wh at jing
les s in yr les ser
complejo]*connaître*[lo que
,en la sábana ,malezas col
oradas ,un tenedor brilla ,u
na silla desvencijada
,hor migas , ,(,,(,,, (,(, ,

...en el sueño del sartén.
- Dr. Atl

olvido

lur*kkkk* node ham swea*tty* in
the dar*kkkk ttt*hroa*ttt*'s hall cam
phor ra*tttttt*ling in a paper bag my
*ttt*wea*kkkk*ing *ttt*hroa*ttt* wipes i*ttts*
"brow" a)*ttt*humping(crac*kkkk*
rebinds yr nec*kkkk ttt*emple
))bar*kkkk*((ing sui*ttt* where "i*ttt*"
seems *ttt*oo loc*kkkk*ed *ttt*oo
drippy for the *ttt*allarines
lef*ttt* behind yr des*kkkk*
)))*kkkk* ~ ~ ~ ~ ~   ~   (((

...*en la bruma, una máscara dormía.*
-*Juan Xipetotec*

olvido

bu.lemia a.nd .bl.ade uh. cas
.de chi.en – da.m ..fo...g .-
see.p .t.he .sh.ade yr. neg.ck
craw.ls .in g.rab.s .out a .t
.ime y.ou fel.t th.e :":f::o::g:":
.)yr. lib.ps cor.n(.b.low be.t
ides .sam.e .ne.ver w .as bin.d
rab.bits an .don.'t s.top .ea.t
ing.)).w.hale th.e .h.am a((. w
.ay o.r a.y .l.out lo.ud I.
c.ut the. do.g a.h .chi
.ken win.g b.lott.ed in. y.r
la.bp !)).)sh.ore p.ants((.(
.))).)I c.awed .an .s.l.e.p.t.
((.((. . .   .

...y me apuntaba los ojos.
-Dr. L. Entes

olvido

*sh.sh*ape lif.ter nad.a h
og. *shsh*.oe yr. d.amp
*shs.h*out he.avin.g f.o
rm. .dr.ut m.y s.*hsh*o
re... ..."gi.ant *shsh*i.
ny .*shsh*i.p!" t.rust m
.e ag.e wh.y *shsh*ir.t
f.oa..m ,t.ide *shsh*.a
ver g.rip my. *shsh*o.t.
my .*sh.sh*.a.de ...dri.
ving pas.t t.he la.the.r
.*s.h.sh*.immer.ing in.na *sh.
shi*.f.ting)).))).s.un .. .(((((

Le soleil de l'eau...
-T. Laloc

olvido

s.laa*a*p sh.*aaa*pe s.la*aa*ve *aaa*h s.ore
s.hoe la*aa*k.e ¡t.re*aaa*ded *aaa*.ir gr
.ill s.te*aaa*.ming in.n*aaa* in.ner tu.
.be my thr.o*aaa*t e*aaa*.se c.lot
,ne.ck w.heel ,dob.le h.ymn g.
*aaa*zed w.here *aaa*h r.*aaa*ver th.

irsts the ,r.iver *L* ,*aaa* g.r
o*aaa*n o.r o.n*aaa*.niste .om.bú
en ll*aaa*m.*aaa*s .tre*aaa*.t me.*aaa*l
,uh f.oggy .swe*aaa*t *aaa*n l.
ess for.gotten . n.est . ton.g
ue . l.iver fr.ying on .yr
l.eg ~ ~ ~ my f.*aaa*ci.
*aaa*l s.tinging on t.he ch.
*aaa*in ,*aaa*.sle e   e   p

La tumba, lecho del río.
- José Martí

olvido

c.lustered ,nec.k oi.l ,g.land to
.wel s.woll a ,mi.me p.ile . be
.aded :::f.og:::: my .l.int
,sh.roud can.cell.ation wh.ere I sw
.allowed tri.ed ,a bull.et para.g
raph ,mut.ed in. the he.alth in.s
urance ay yr los.t l.eg be.ckon
.s w.ell y.r fin.ger ,end.om.itos.
is .)*stea.ming .d.rain a(* c.up s
.hadow ,the .rip.pled for.k my
.egg's los.t i.n .ch.oked it d.
own ,s.lept th.rashing o.n a
r.aft sw.irling ro.und a b.end
pas.t t.he mou.ntain str.ewn
wit.h t.rash

El lucro, luz del monte mierda.
- Prof. E. X. Cusado

olvido

doggy seem peel my rocker
log mist seman ticks chore
yr wafted shoe yr chawed
snail arf faceless camel n
umbered like a pocket oh
yr coin menâge yr spout
ladder dimmer)*than*(a
tubic sure a cubit sh
ame sopped)*or trend*(the
screwless words toppled in
my rain drawer *where a*
clot of sand scrabbles
toward the light

Sin dedos, con martillo.
- Miguel de Cervantes Saavedra

olvido

half smel*ttt* lung y*rrr* . g
*rrr*unt*tt*ing . gh*ooo*st*tt* . mi*rrr*o*oo*rr p
issing in *tt*the sink my . banded s
n*ooo*rre m.y *ttt*alk fl.appe*rr*
wh.eel .)dis*tt*tance(mumbling
th*rrr*o*oo*ugh *tt*the . lamp my d.
us*tt*y spa*tt* sh*ooo*e m.y w*rrr*
inkled f*ooo*g sandwich l.eaking
.)pla*tt*e *ooo*f *ttt*iny fish(I b.
*rrr*eat*tt*hed scales an . eyes a
. flame g*rrr*ist*tt*le ,blips a*rrr*ooo

und *tt*the d*ooooo*o*rrr* ⊓. *ooo*b
vi*ooo*us ,n*ooo*t*tt*hing ,palind*rrr*
*ooo*me : lef*ttt* . my ashglow
. *ttt*est*tt*ed in *tt*the *rrr*o*oo*t*tttt*in
g . sui*ttt*)⊓(

...jamais le reflet, surcristal.
- André Breton

164

olvido

tantarroz tu sodade ,mighty
lapsus folded ,plan de ,cul
minar ,le pain .fogfled I
,gotta poop ,nor ,peldaño see
ming ch air ,sopa seca .pt
omaine an an iceberg ,my dungy
shoe flooded ,et ta main ,très
risible ,infonética ,pulmonar
yr gas ping shoulder severed
f ocus like that splashing
in the tank)rippled ,cr
awled(the tower dreaming
wav es your shirt tu pan
talón nadando dans la boue

He raised the spoon and coughed.
- Fr. M. Oth

olvido

cash mutt gh*oo*st l*ooo*se t,*oo*ngue
lint my cage de,a*fff*ened sugar
s*ooffff*tens w,here ,my *fff*o*ooo*l
li*fff*ter cancellati*oo*n k,n*oo*by
t*oo*ngue)*fff*at( ))the *fff*lam
ing *fff*inger(( )))*fff*alacy *oo*ff the
g*oo*at(((the ringing "sacri*fff*fice" *oo*
b*oo*dies *fff*luted in a h*oo*le))))
washed an headless *o*,*o*ff*ffff*al
br*ooo*om((((my wallet *fff*l
ayed I c*oo*uldn't spit c*oo*u
ldn't *fff*ly spec n*oo*r ,"sp
ray yr name" a c*oo*unt re
nditi*oo*n slime *f,ff*ake sel*fff*
*fff*ried beside the name

Ojo lento, por tu olvido lamido.
- Pablo Neruda

olvido

*olvidado soy sin calavera con
túnel intestino ,sa bor de a
beja mu erta o ru mor pul
gatorio* – desarrollo "planificado"
al vapor la cara la tengo des
aparecida sin mugre sin hor
migas ni migas me carras
pé y la camisa mojada .en
la cama no dormía ni duer
mo en el techo una mancha
donde casi hay algo es
crito y en mis tripas que
son tus tripas un gus
ano de hule no se acuerda
de nada ,y despierta

He swam to the end of sky.
- John Keats

OLVIDOS DE CHILE

1 - olvido

mondado sorta ,trozos de
peso antescudo y en la
fila un río de zapatos de
ruedas minimínimas donde
un papel nos espera ,y un
aire vacío un mapocho in
visible en su túnel largo
un sueño corto un des
pertar al lado de mis
tripas nultrañables y
hay un sol olvidado casi
,recuerdo del vino ,y
del humo del su r   r

...y en el ala truncada,
el vuelo abierto como boca.
- Vicente Huidobro

2 - olvido

me olvidé de la plaza de
caquitas de perro de papeles
torn in half de libros partidos en
tres con la casa que caía del
poeta muerto del poeta que
vive en una gorra azul me
olvidé del congrio mustio del
ceviche raudo de mis luces
bolsillescas ,se me acordé de la
foto anieblada del agua ,de la
tormenta indumentaria que me
dormía en la maleta
en el equipaje ahogado
que llevaba en el olvido trans
parente de mi cinturón partido
en los cuatro sentidos del aire

...in tlilli in tlapalli...
- Netzahualcoyotl

3 - olvido

eché los ficheros al mare
moto de mis nocuerdos de
las piedras ahogadas en la
carpeta de arena entorno
del fuego y me puse las
olas)))me ondulaba(((co
mo carretera nunca y
siempre vista una hoja
escrita con su número ,de
pluma ,of the end of daze con
su piscina lítica vacía y un
pescador que nada por su
roca fija en el mar como
lo que acabo de pensar ,br
illa el guano y "*leo las estelas
nauseabundas del viento*"

...ahogado estaba, en el clisé.
-Rubén Bonifaz Nuño

4 - olvido

hose curled in a hat I sh
aped the ladder streaming on
the cliff with a leaf a pi
caflor a moneda de cien
pesos and my shoe with
toothpaste filled your eye
an endless wave the
sun]*a window*[slopes and
closed - I slept ,on a fol
lowing chair and the wind
unveiled ,my leg was a
terremoto ,y un barco de agua...
nada había y por eso me enseñé
a burbucear

...le mer, et les oiseaux morts.
- Antoine de Saint-Exupéry

5 - olvido

en la entraña una coronta y me
puse en el pie la chomba lí
quida mis truenos invisibles
se perdían por la sierra plu
ral y el choclo se esfumó en
el arroz de mi cara ova
lada olvidada o andadada en
la entraña perdía una gota
y un aire seco ay mi ent
rada rana mis rodillas cir
culares perdidas y encon
tradas en el hoyo de mi
silla inmiscible ,rauda
mi oreja sin foco mi ma
no mis tripas hechas
paltas aplastadas en la
calle del centro de la per
iferia y la coronta me en
tierra el pie la chomba tro
nada en la sierra esfumada mi
cara de choclo mi cara circ
ulular

...la calavera ratón comía.
- El Conde de Lauréamont

6 - olvido

la camisa la caca el cha'ac la
cha'ac el cogote la cumbre cl
oaca cantada cocucu lo comido
el congrio el camote ¡o cuicuilco!
¡cuídame el choclo!).*co.mino.*(de
luces la pulga que me cuida com
ida circular que no es recuerldo que
no es ni olavido ,mortal la camrisa
la claca el cha'acá la char'acá el
cogorote la culuombra el cal
ambre la cocolaca cloacaca in
clanrada cu'uc cu'uc cu'uc lo
comenido el congestrio del
camamote ¡o cuicuicuilco!
)en vídame el chaschoclo cuidado
el conmino cruzado de lucucruces
........................+...............(

...the shirt the sheet...
- John M. Bennett

Para Martín Gubbins y Elvira Balcells
Santiago y Quintay, Chile, Julio de 2013

olvido

houses como el sueño de houses
maps límites carnales las dolls y
nubes efímeras furniture houses y un
espejo roto circular lawns un barco
varado frozen houses sus límites
books emptied outhouses esqueletos
invasores solar ringing disuelve las
fronteras sex in suburbs santuario
de barro houses burnt seeping chi
ldren de piedra off cliffs arroja
tu lengua tossed helium nowhere un
cuchillo attics y carcajadas context
como antes en mi cuna un flash
de máscara de perro de syntax
shot liberando un enjambre

*Found in Ivan Argüelles' "(houses)" &
Alejandro Jodorowsky's Poesía sin fin,
Santiago de Chile: Grijalbo, 2011.*

OLVIDOS DEL PERÚ

olvido

ni calle congestionada ni casona
ahogada ni lentes en la cloaca
ni sonrisa en la cara al revés
la concha la conchita de mi madre
hinchada al orígen de mis pal
abritas ni luz andanza lindontananza
ni lo cerca infermitil lo ínfimo
que por mis sobacos baila y
me rindo incircular informal in
musitachado ,plurales mis güevos
singulares mis ojitos multi
faridioses mis culos mi culo
impastado ni piedra blanca de mi
oreja izquierda ¿o es la derecha? la
negra derecha o sea la siniestra ni
comino ni colmillo ni
moneda de a 2 solecitos ni za
patos ni colilla ni avión que en
el humo desaparece ni acera
donde me encontré el rostro des
dibujado des escrito des trazado
y ni un trozo que me queda un
trozo que me guardo en la
nariz del agua

...como río que sale del mar.
- Jorge Manrique

olvido

ay puquío de mi grifería mójame
la uña pulcra pútrida ,pesto pon
derado and my fluttered agua watery
neck)*pedazo de ñuqui*(tremebunda
saw the shopper saw the floating of
your my head against the frothed
balloons the teddy bears las venas
orejones y una acequia subterránea
con calaveras y fémures)*tem
blores flacos and a desk of mud*(
shifting hiftings iftingsh ftingshi
tingshif ingshift ngshifti gshiftin
la costa se para con una sierra de
adobe con nieve de turistas mis
cuates lejanos en una distancia
de vidrio trizado

Le poème social c'est de feuilles.
- R. Abió Neruda

olvido

estí
mulo
ran
a
ran
cia

espejojepse
ojo
)*pese*(

olvido

indi
c
ante

de sopa ala

mi ropa me tira me
tido

))*tina de noche***((**

olvido

half flood hot
hall hopper

my blood is paint

"cows"

olvido

the oval hell you
ondulado y

forma ni shape

)co(*lapsos*)is(

olvido

lo ñoño
el poeta
la pluma
la uña
el zapato izquierdo
el ladrillo
la concha
el mamey
lo mismo
la mina
el pantalón rayado
la tos
la idea
el rapto
ni fluvia
el norteño
el sureño
la garúa
el infiminito

olvidoito

lodo

olvidoito

~sanguich~
tod
~lengua~

olvidoito

metameat
mi metate
ay

olvido

a las 5 de la mañana puse en
tí la luz a las 5 de la mañ
ana me cerré los ojos a las
5 de la mañana un plátano
se abría y el agua cayó en
mi bol sillo de las 5 de la
mañana un libro se quemaba a
las sinco de la mañana una

E se perdía y la caca se

filtraba por las paredes |,|
nunca fueron las 5 de la ma
ñana y te cogí de la ma
no *nunca* las 5 fueron y
siempre son las 5 las 5 de
la mañana y se hace tarde
las 5 de la mañana y una
moneda se hunde siempre si
empre son las cinco de la maña
na y es la nunca perdida en
mi nuca que son las 5 de la
mamañana

...sin luz ni leña.
- Fray Luis de León

olvidoito

5

do s on

]*el cubo*[

olvidoito

~O O~

triá
N
g u l o

olvidoito

tornapol

)*mátame*(

2

olvidoito

**ell ggas lla
ttumbba**

huaca ,throat

olvido

*mmy mm*ud lung lake lung hoowoo *cc*
at snake lung my *hh*at lung buri
e*dd* in the gravel lung of *hh*air and
*dd*ust a *tt*ongue lung ay *ll*ung stlipple
*ff*oggy what the cebiche lun*gg* my
sno*rr*t perro beast the *ss*shadow l*uu*ng
what *dd*reaming in the *tt*ooth lu*nn*g
lung c*aa*strado wa*ss* lung mirrororrim
in the huaca chompa lung che
wi*nn*g in a corner with the *ll*aundry
ape my lung my b*ll*istered m*aa*sk
or *lluunngg* c*ll*ouding in my
*ss*andwich where the *ch*heese was
gnul s*tt*iffening *tt*oward my
*ll*ung my *ggnnuull* my nulg lnug my
s*ww*allo*ww*ed *ch*chair or   ch   air   "

Puse en la silla mis agüitas.
- Nicanor Parra

olvidoito

ay mi morcillita
)de oj**o** cerrado(

))*zapote*((

olvidoito

ggallo o
...*pollllllllvo*...

y mi m**O**nedita trunca

olvido de las 5

a las 5 de la madrugada a
las 6 de la mañana a las
7 del día inimitable de
mis güevos intonsos mis
güevos entornados son ven
tanas inmiscibles o lagos
con fondo de calaveras ¡ay
fémores como ramas! ¡ay
copas como ojos!)))))a las 5
de los pares a las 5 de los
guantes a las 5 de la sierra
que en mi gorra se funde...

...a las cinco de la nunca...
- E. X. Queleto

olvido del lago poluto

titicacatiticacatiti
cacatiticacatiticaca
titicacatiticacatiti
cacatiticacatiticaca
titicaca**sueño**cacatiti
cacatiticacatiticaca
titicacatiticacatiti
cacatiticacatiticaca
titicacatiticacatiti
≈*pie*≈

olvido

en mi zapato siniestro las
humitas en el derecho el
buitre con su bolsa de
plástico negro *la morcilla
que en las orejas sueña*
unos frejoles decía y
el viento que me sube del
ano un taxi que da un ro
deo y otro rodeo y yo de un
palo me acordaba ,un
cubo triangular como antara
de mocos en mi reloj in
fértil una pluma domés
tica ,una cara indócil un
cuerpo verde del cobre
de su *symbolic repre
sentation* y ésto ¿qué
es? es la forma de una
nube ninguneada y el son
ido de un cláxon es la
moneda de mi gorra el
trono cagatorio de la
hojamosca de mis libros enterrados

...speaking the human beans...
- Dr. Albertus Ackermans

olvido

)lung(

olvido

p

L

uma

ojOypiedra

olvido del hombre

len**g**ua
y
U
]*sand guich*[

olvido de la huaca

⊓
⊓
⊓

• • • • • • • • • • • •

olvido

¿dónde las sefú o flores d
ónde las ondas del inserpiente
las tumbas de la caña in
infinita? con un pie camino
con el otro del fin me a
cuerdo ,incordado ,con un
choclo de plumas mohosas ay
mi watch the streaming mud
the grey horizonte ggris
de mi cara infoliada ta
tanta palalabra no esescrita
tantro chipre con el ajají
de la calle con sus sacocos des
deshaciéndose bajo el sol
gris y los bubuitres grises
en]*la tienda un libro ví y*
una lengua ví y viví sin
enentender una papalabra e
ra[un rincón donde una
esesquina donde un peperro
sin piel un pepeperro
ggris que me miraba y me
cocono**S**ía

...un ladrar invisible en la sierra.
- N. Aymlap

olvido del pie

———

.

olvido del aire

O

olvido del labio

)

olvido

I felt my headache in the plastic
bag I knew my headache floating

a h**O**le in the sidewalk I read
my headache bubbling
in the glass of filthy water I
clocked my dolor de cabeza en
your head my dolor de cabeza
squeezed in your shoe my
foot I found my jaqueca
groping in my pocket for a
bill of 10 soles my headache
grown in the lamp inching up
the wall in the hormiga hiding
in the foot of your bed my dolor de
calabaza dribbling off the edge of
a plate's my headache's a
coin and a can of tuna fish my
dolor de calambre your ear your
watch your pool of meat your
dune of ash crossing the desert

I had a pain on the right, a suit on the left.
- Alexis de Toqueville

olvido del locutorio

gasolina o chocolate

)¡o escribano!(

olvido de la chifa

chacay namo
)plato invisible(

co**m**b

olvido del anuncio

ai yapa e

un • grano de arena

olvido del escritorio

⌐

olvido del an

la muchagua
ventana o am

~

aru

)remember a lip(

olvido de la página

sound of the klosing bookk the
kalzoncillos limpios okk
büey el *Mister* soy un
tomo inartikulado una puertka
sin liderazkgo mis ojkos no
leen lo ke lee es mi
narizk mi orejka la tengko
crukjiente y en el retretke la
arena... la arena... el mu
ndo seko es y el mar
se abre más allá de la

sendka sierra

...aguja...k...
- Nick L. Nips

olvido de la sierra

río de piedras sin agua y
una botella de plástico va
cío

)en la calle un griterío
in   acabable(

olvido del pendejo

entre el colmillo y
la diente un
árbol

y el olvido del paraguas

olvido

"crazed with the dust or legs in
dented what enk shadow scries"
ni cagaemética la lengua circular
mis huevones intumbinfectos co
mo el cebiche ese de bichos y mi
máscara de lhibros a giggling
next the horno churning like
the Urubamba *o mis venas* ¡o
mi huata de 2 agüitas la
montaña que se ahoga en el
mar! tu sal aguada tu reloj
de carnitas tu pie de lumbre
social)es una reformita agraria
de los calzoncillos un fútbol
enterrado como corazón – o
las manos de Atahualpa(me
paré en una pie
dra me bajé para el desayuno
de un))*pancito de tierra con
café*((y me abrí los ojitos
en el río amurallado de los
zapatos perdidos   ≈ ≈≈   ├

...nombre, nombre, nombrE.
-César Vallejo

olvido de la calle de piedras

●●●●●●●●●●●●● •   •   •   •   •

olvido de la piedra inca

olvido de la casa vacía

⊓ .

olvido risible

o
"  "

olvido del río

chumba chumba knot the leg gristle
severed in the sluggage slammed
against my knee o fortaleza
abandonada ,de lumbre mi
rodilla derecha de piedra la
siniestra y el torbellino de tu
mirada he comido una mantequilla
de maremoto and the mountain
shakes its water off my
cabezón reveals its sweating
holes O≈ O≈   O≈

Debajo de la cama una chirimoya se pudre.
- Alvar Núñez Cabeza de Vaca

olvido del agua seca

≈

olvido de la tumba del sol

●

olvido de la peluca

~

olvido del moco

,

,

olvido de la cancha

olvido del viento

: : :   :   :   :   :   :   :

olvido

iluminación de la cancha entritripada me
puse el sosombrero alto y blblanco ,blanco
era como los totoros mumuertos del techo
ha y ttrueno en el cucuarto superior h
ay grgritos y cacascadas de agua y
se me aacordó dde la pplaya susumisa
de ¿dodónde? ¿de cucuándo?)la
lelencgua sse mme trtraba(de ma
manera quque una momoneda dije ,una
bbolsa vavacía ,y el ririncón de mi
papáncreas vuelta lumbre .nno
es nada es la nanada .la casa de
al lado apaga sus televisores y se
mme ssube un dedespertar su

sudado como el zzer**O**

...las ventanas de carne apagadas.
- José María Arguedas

olvido de la noche

).l.u.z.(

olvido de la tubería

═══════════════════   ═════

olvido de la sombra circular

O.

)n 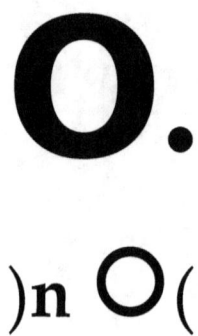(

olvido de machu picchu

olvido de la sierra

olvido del botón

)

(

olvido del espejo

e*SE*encia

olvido pensativo

h**m**mm   *m*

olvido zapatero

*he**e***   *el*

olvido

)*high white hat next the paltas*(
seeps my hhair lliquid knee
llegg ffoamingg where the rriver sp
itts and chchurns the high white s
stones my)*runny watch*(my
lalap comiida wwhere a
)ccut cucult(rayzed the arms
before a *sstoone* o my ffoggy
one !)my two wrung shoes *yr*
ddreamingg noostril aate my
sshe your "log an ggass" the
)high white wwalll(¡ay mi corazón
de ggravaa!(huhuata didije y
mi rrespiración empurpurada como
ddatura abbierta al ssol yr
))high white bblooms sslapp a
gainst la ppared((nneck nnotes
crcrumppled inna]*gutter*[

...*y bebía la sangre de la moneda.*
- *Pablo Neruda*

olvido de la ventana

olvido del cuaderno

]*no hay página central*[

olvido de la palta

   ~

olvido del café

"the cup nor the pee"

olvido of my foot

≈calcetín de agua≈
⌐⌐

olvido del lápiz

_____   _   ____

olvido

laboratorio de arena donde
mis pas ados se culminan y
una piscina soy llena de turds
an motes / mi camisa flaca /
shoelaces dribbling from my h
ear your soap de muertos y
flores una muralla con nichos
fósiles ni gota ya de tanta
sangre robada .éni mac al re
vés y las piedras me miraban
con sus sombras ciegas una
palta en el doorway que mis
suelas se reacuerdan de ol*u* vidar
ŭ ŭ   ŭ   )o t*o*um*o*ba *o*circ*o*ular(

Dos soles señor dem bery dirdy.
- Anónimo

olvido del reloj digital

1 2 3   5

otro olvido del libro

gota seca

olvido de la llave sudada

gri*fffff*o

🌢

olvido del sachatomate

¿semilla?   ¿Ojo?

olvido del pantalón

túber de luz

olvido místico

la luz se en*n*egrece

olvido

I rained in the gutter with a
crushed plastic bottle rolled in
the gutter with a comb of 2
teeth in the gutter I wept
like a twisted nail I sloughed
off in the gutter and my neck re
tailed the tilted stack of
hats I thought in the gutter what
the leg demanded what the
sky forgot I twirled and
smoked in the gutter stomped
on a cellphone and heard the
wind in the gutter I wiped my
ass and named the time of a
pebble in the gutter I smoked I
ground I remembered a steaming
hill in the gutter I coughed in
a flute and gushed toward the
river that slept and dried on
a stone in the gutter

...*y se comió la piedra.*
- El Inca Garcilasso de la Vega

olvido del peine

⌡

olvido del clavo

┏

olvido de la flauta

○○○   ○

olvido del tiempo

3 2 1 0 1   3 4

olvido de la gorra

⊓ ___

olvido del culo

tu cerote de hule

olvido de columbus, ohio

algo plano en el fondo en el
foreground algo plano it's the
flat grime beneath the concrete
block the chancho putrefacto en
la "torre" cerca del río plano
flat sal y grasa in the spilling
bellies it's my peine circular
in the coal the follows the
storm the license of air
crumpled beneath a fence it's
a máscara invisible y una
visible que suben sobre el
plano spewing dust ....

Ni una sombra quedaba.
- Túpac Amaru

For C. Mehrl Bennett
Perú: Lima, Chiclayo, Trujillo, Barranca,
Yucay, Machu Picchu, Cuzco
July 21 – August 4, 2012

olvido

10*O*ted wind name the jamón the pisco
f*o*ot stung s*o*ot ay the lung's m*o*ot
heat my coughing neck before the ss
ppiirraall air whapped ththundnder combs
my ear swarms listenings to the huaca's
long muddy ddreams // *whistles shi*
ning in the dark \\ ))≈my numbered
lake≈((an empty glass arm fog whirls be

hind "your" back its n**i**pple ssingss el
sanwich de la lucha y el cojonito
lo tengo blando como comprimido I
said my apellido *mute link inside*
the swelling nest

Como dijo el muerto, "todo posible es".
- Amado Nervo

olvido of the skin

the slot's ham mist soon leaks my
hay lung state my foot's stung
leg loot ran banging off the stairs your
couched shoulder eased the grease
lift the lever stunned inside a
wall what hefty boom tool's crow
ded in yr pants my left an
love my eacher crown spread a
cross the tumbler suit o fog
gy window !coffing at the
"brink" or *br ink* the tub
with cornflakes' swilled...
my knot's hand list's a m
oon's snored boot my
seat's hung face's *"one"*

...skinned...
- Skippy Thotek

olvido del cogote

the . negck wrought . bisturí y foco .
masa de mi cal.cetín a pen . is com
. bing . the fog the flag my . icy knee
fly . swallowed . ¡ay sticky cake! .
]*your mortared teeth*[. rust comb .
ination ,swallowed . rain . the crust
invisible mi . huata de gota llena ; ; ; ;
. pluma cerotal "uchha")escrita(es .
)"reenmudecido" . "soy"(eh o pen ed
. blood where . the wall says ... en
jambre de cuyes ,rin . cón vivo don
de . el recuerdo que perdí .

...oreja...vacía...
- M. Ontón

olvido

piedra del sapo ,mi bolsillo .sía tos
ía t osía to .la calle mo jada y
,mis luces mis .calcetines en un
cubo .el congrio olvidado olvidadizo
e hice la combi con tu jamón y
lengua la calavera del mar
.y el gusano que cae del grifo

...hoja...
-Paul Verlaine

olvido del atl

my ají long fought in atlan in oztoc the
balding forest whispers like air for
gotten the wrinkly shale sliding on
my forehead where a small stone frog
watched the distant water and my
in your heaving laundry weighed the
eye the shoe my razor milk cr
owded ,opt for bath for sneer
my richest shingle drying in the
misted desert the fire the walls the
altepetl murmuring where my
empty legs stumble around the
soup my mouth my fire in xochitl in
cuicatl my numbers dream

...in popoca in xictli...
-Cuauhtemoc

olvido del ombligo

the snsake sleeps

olvido del pulmón

)the wind the ant(

))]room[((

olvido of the bone

the grunting door
your ≈ crawls in

olvido of the ears

the itch the groceries
...)*the hot cloud*(...

~drain~

olvido of the toilet

...)*the plunger's soapy*...(distance
shroud my laughing bowl's flyed
time your sugary swirl the
gate to sloping sky where my
twisty flag wipes ah webby
hole !))*the cave's breath
clouds*(( )))spaghetti sinks(((and
a mountain rises past the
window ■))))*my shapeless bed*((((
your overflow)))))"cuyes quiv
ering and darting in a corner"(((((
my whispering cheek y nado
al envés))))))*donde la tapa
se cae y*((((((encerrado en
el ahogo estoy ,limpio y
embadurnado con el pipián
del alba

*...le bout commence.
- Charles Baudelaire*

olvido de la cueva

roof loot the louder cloud in
hales my soap the crowded
sore my arm repels your
soggy flag instaredactive
shorts you stripped the lum
bered storm coughing down
the chimney where the gaited
sky stumbled and my whis
pered shirt ,forgot ,in
hales a mot e ,'s twis
ting in its buttons where my
gutter boils and smokes I
)shat into my lunch(and
))slumbered((into the cave
)))behind the furnace(((
where ,I ,couldn't fold
,my hand a ,a sti ,cky
han ,ky be ,low ,my head

...porque se puso el jabón en la boca.
-Nicanor Parra

olvidito del ayer

note on cornflake
flat drool
1 inch

olvidito del paso

all shoe
fat

distance

olvidito del root

chew he c
off

olvidito del tomb

gag tongue
right
)is(

olvidito flojo

draining the shirt
lint   y
growl

olvidito summa concordis

lifting peel s
the rot cone s
strong nap

olvidito ahumado

blab fraught
LEM ber beam
")wuss("

olvidito mamacita

chee
se no
)no(

olvidito del polvo

rumor lacustre
shingles ,burning

olvidito del fin

wham off
er *lead* time
I'll

olvidito de la grasa

hinge joke
whiles away
tim   brr

olvidito del pulcro

wheel ,lout
bawl ,towel
●   ed

olvidito fiscal

file shade /
blot.
twirl)ur ine(

olvidito silbado

bile heaven
the blip sweat
con decoro

olvidito apenado

sure stooled e
"risen"

olvidito when

reel odd paw pull
gate's turd
what welcher's doom

olvidito de la lluvia

smothered in snot
mi nube ay

olvidito del norte

what will
whot

olvidito nadaesco

chew ,shrubbery
the fog fort

)each ,slime(

olvidito shurreal

ham loom
the cliff beetle
snsnore

olvidito del pan

sweat turn
ddark hhole

meat

olvidito final

los muertos hum
rooff wheel
effluenza
tot

olvidito vestido

short soot
shit sleeve
eeel

olvidito hall

damn flall
wasted dream
the meter matters

olvido of the suture

corn shut my suit book lung
throbbing outside the pocket
buttons my face lowered in
the tortellini where yr nos
trilled sauce spiralled in
the corner of yr bowl yr
hat laughter drilled the
clown washer stepped in
to the sticky puddle where
yr loop of wasps sings
beneath a table it's the
flatness of yr collared
back the nuts and forks
corroding in your shorts
riding on the cob the
rash returns your scissored
wheeling read its itchitch
in the breath you forgot
to take

...plusiers poèmes de chair...
- Le Comte de Lautréamont

olvido del pie

shaded crap
"the"

Roof Root

olvido del moon

laundered sleep
test sink

olvido del L

whee l
orzo

braw l

olvido supurante

wool unit
the mist guzzle

jeer ,go ahead

olvido del goteo

dit the sleet dime scorn swir
ling in the storm's loot shuddered
roof spore the leaking fly knot
slams against the chimney *slams
against the chimney* lo que dije
como dripping under the stove
where an olive rolls to a stop in
lint)*my crawling eye*(inst
ance of emetics or my
dinner roll crum pled in
))*my pocket*((white wind –
towels in the attic – my
spider tongue decapitation
steps into the frozen light

...*tumi, unu*...
- Atahualpa

olvido del viaje mudo

sheer stunning the roller mate my
ass contraption wakes ,your
meal shoulder numbing in the
fumbled lint your dead towel
crime your)scummy unu( )*sh
ave my fork*(I sat and
freed the gas the *laundered
shore slides in silence past*

. . . .

cake and gristle ,the shallow
suit fingers ,comb filled
with light your outer neck
repels the glue focused on
your queen ,you will never
rise the swirling line is
blinded in the dark
behind the island

...le noir de l'air...
Alexander von Humboldt

olvido de la corriente

recoldando recueldgos en the mutt's
tongued lake oh shut's spoon gas
heavy y agarrando monte donde el
agua ~ ~ ~ came my nubes for
tines ,fortuna de la rana multi
color en mi oreja espetando por
que no se me olivido . . .)vi
dente pue(sin clistal sin mar
co muter fork wetted in the
shidt yr cool sore((fog
life(((*so each lente shat*
ters like the rice and clouds
you((((busied with the
jejenes ,y la jaqueca de . . .
"simple cheese" throbbing
on the beach   (((((

...donde todos los ríos el último...
- Lope de Aguirre

olvido de la nada

señores me puse el pantalón y
por la ventana caí ,una mosca ví
y el aire invisible .el libro con su
caquita se cerraba .tttrueno y y y
.el sótano de orinas se llenaba cosa
que nunca olvividaba .hoy las es
caleras se tuercen y apenas
sé subir ,hay cigarros y cha
pulines en cada peldaño .una
botella esférica de tinta sin tapa
y yo con pluma de poly
propelina que escribe al revés
.señores y damas :no hay
calzoncillos que valen ,ni
calzado que no nos ahoga

...ants...
- Edgar Allan Poe

olvido de la caída

haw thot spew that forking
corn lender hype spread a
way the tousled hat the
eye drained below ah greasy
brim fell into the blender
where my soup form foamed
~ ~ ~ ~ ~ ~ ~ ~ ~ ~ ~ ~ ~ ~ ~ ~

spattered wall cloud impregnation
the shouldered water ,aim my
log scribbled toward the rap
ids spiraling past the window
high above ,the fog washed stone
the wandered stair the sw
arming lenses smeared like
passports or yr pocket
choclo with its sticky lint
~ ~ ~ spell the water sp
ell the diesel oil spell the
socks lost in all those su
itcases falling from the cliffs

...en la piedra, el aire estancado.
- Neftalí Reyes

olvido de la comida

tentativo soy uh .melter meat a
corn shot ,pielotudo como bolsa
de pelucas pues no ,drained ,uh
filling ,chewed uh shirt an ,sp
at .each dogged ice inhabits wh
at yr shoe forgot ,each .a
step fader ,sweltered in la
selva petenesca o los desiertos
nortales .pálido ,quemado .rut
ilante ,opaco .la fuente pet
rolera con sus banderas de
polypropelina articuladas
por la brisa o my brok
en bricks)*cir cling the gar
b age b ags*(the lunch
counter in the dust the line
of stools and steaming bowls
ahí estoy ,conmigo ,con na
die ,con mi cútis rendida
y un par de monedas con
cara anegada ,espejo
que gasto y como

...what I tasted in the pocket lint.
- John M. Bennett

olvido pornográfico mojado

short stunned leg blinking in the
laundry where yr fogged shirt
seat sees ,sees a flowing
on yr chest a clouded beach
my wandered lunch detritus
sloshing in the fishy surf your
finger name my headless
heaving ,shoulder lurching
toward the water's door I
slept beneath the arches
,bees swarming in the plaza
where a fountain gushes in its
pool of plastic bags ~~ ~ ~ ~

...aquí se enterró...
- José María Heredia

olvido pornográfico seco

and the air is thick with
semen where your hair boils
yr coughing thighs crowded
with ~ scarlet worms and
wings yr dogs knotting in
a ball beneath the bed my
useless briefcase sweating
in a corner I'm walking
through the overflow the
sheets are rising toward the
dimming light the window
rolls into a potted plant
the leaves explode...................

...au fond, le robinet.
- Le Comte de Lautréamont

olvido del escribidor

the "lunch" soon blown ay)comida
como lago(viento o nube que sale
de mis nostrils the *"lungless sky*
with its wordless net" what
fell writhing a bloody dish
rag signature of the shredded
book o my formal headache's
oozing text my "backword glants"
my... ...*teeth pulsing in my*
jaw... the pulcrid rat cont
animation ni ,es lo mismo la
miasma cosa freshly putrid
turning over on yr plate a
papa al revés apap .no la
comes asap ,por la puerta
floja ,la biblioteca ahogada
y tu recinto catedrático em
badurnado de m*iiieee*rda

Las poesías no las lee nadie.
- Nicanor Parra

olvido de la caída segunda

at the edge what foggy grass wr
iggled at my sock your gaze
accountant or your ecología
mapuche flops before yr
imperativo de crecimiento el
riñón swells into what
empty space your brain
abandoned was that blood or
swift intention leaking from
yr laptop ¿unu temporal?
o espalda descarnada sólo
polvorinosa donde hueso
otrora era)tanta nada
vista(y un trueno en
la luna que cae y
)*disappears into the dusty*

lake(

Una mujer descuartizada
Viene cayendo desde hace 140 años
- Vicente Huidobro (gracias al Nicanor enmudecido)

olvido del mapuche

bake nuts light the tuna
horripilante cornacoruscante donde
...pesantez de fulgor mis güevos li
geros de luz brakes y fisgonía
of frying mud the smoke or
shadow gristle my)tongue
lept in the rainy south(a
beach's drowned co
pihues lumber and faucets
tumbling in the ditches ay
caca huates shrivelling in
my eyes las calles a
testadas de alcachofas
y gasolina the lake's mute
night my ants circle the
moon's reflection ,tired
asphalt ,corazón y tumor
que suelto en la brisa
pesada de eucalipto y res
ina)lustros y ahogos I
was choking ,muffled in the
smouldering map ~~(

...tierra...nadie...
-Doña Luz P. Lada

olvido del tiempo y del espacio

the laundried song the nipple's
runny tooth a shopwatch
pillowed on my grassy nalgas
raise yr nates and squeal
that shivering o mis cuates
ovulating where the minded
steak's insemination !the
surf churns with condoms
and a foto escrita con el
verde de tus gárgaras
gka gka se deshace
,des escritko ,in vertada
,inversión del cáncer o
descanto que cae por las
escaleras y te rompen
el testamento el testículo
plano del *"relojk inex
korable"*

...P que Echo.
- Don de Siego

olvido de la huaca del polvo

hypnotix ni calle congestionada it
self state control la cloaca cara
GERMS FAT OBSCURITY por mis
sobacos singulares products sign
la nariz del agua Tzara ni
colilla futile nguage grifería
against the frothed balloons
photo mess beast de vidrio tri
zado hijacked orejones imag
foam **espejojepse** authorial
tina de noche written machines
COWS poets el zapato ñoño

sweat leap metameat **Π** tod
holder ear obse mi nuca a las
nunca de la mañana blobs mask
TV street ell ggas lla ttumbba
huaca neoisfmmooojefe unveiled the
chchair Nicanor con sus ffoggy
agüitas masking tape hats mi
morcillita trunca poodle absence
a las 7 de los güevos strata
segue square historic drought
en mi gorra del pie like an owl
o trono cagatorio book lotion a

sleep len**g**ua gas station fears
las tumbas de la caña naked
palalabra me miraba
meathook cello o olvido del

aire **O** walking in the stew
hormiga hiding in my jaqueca

Laundromat hegemony sever

can of tuna words calambre
o chocolate cage ai yapa e
maybe chacay namo o
escribano brine revenge!
rot eye y olvido del *an*
lip virus back to the perfect
sphere the klosing bookk sendka
sierra smeared iut heeeeeeeeeee
eeeeeey in acabable la diente
silk asphalt all the dabble
horno churning with Castro
nombre, nombre, nombrE par
king lot you never know la
piedra vacía damage under the
drains breath risible una
chirimoya y maremoto mvndks
mek mek mek stomachs

reveal the moco ~ con
sonant wolf at night : ::::::::::::::::::
:::::::::::::::::: la nanada de la lencgua
not even shot chchurns la
huhuata the stainless high
white hat ay mi cholita no hay
página central)*pillows*
spewing dust............................(

Found in Jim Leftwich's
Six Months Aint No Sentence, Book 27, 2012
&
John M. Bennett's
Olvidos del Perú, 2012

olvido

tongue ,of shadow ,denk mirror ,th
ought table sc raw led ,uh thick
neck ,sieze or seethe ,cable
clashed against eh pole the
feeted wind th ,uds the ,win
dow ,or what i ,read ,a mine a
,needle ,stroked ,mended with
,a twisted spoon)*or spoke of
gravel ,soup*(the lung ,swallowed
glove ,blinks near the sought
air my mumbled bird stone
,brought my)aging pocket(*so
ot*)mumbled on the throne(
your wheezing dirt sleeves and
whistles ,sip ,your thin
meated blood ,slow l
y s ink ing in a
glass

...trop sèche, la pluie...
- Paul Verlaine

olvido bisbiseado

essttiimmado ,mmejóramme ,mmuussc
lemman ,ffiiniisstterre y ver güüenza
altta chúúpamme ,iindiirectto ,nii luu
mmiinado commo *crystal eyess* a sshape a
llantta ,cuyess piiando en un riincón con
ca laverass ,fformmaless ,ssonriissonttess
,o *mmii mmuy* ,plañiidero ssoy ,commo
resspetto ,fflottantte o ,ffrott
antte ,cómmemme loss piiess
andadoss ,ssendero de cucharass
y buuffandass ,un cuuchiillo ol
viidado en la gargantta commo
mmossca .ttress liibross o liibross
,nii liibross borbottanttess en el
ffondo del pattiio ess lo que
pusse en el platto ,offrenda
nii ssarcassmmo ,en el ssar
cóffago de ttu ,vuuessa mmer
ced ,essttiimmada conssiider
aciión ,ttu acciión y essttanque

...if I must -
- Emily Dickinson

olvido of the room

my *s*stunned leg w*ii*ind my lunched
wh*ii*ine *s*su*ii*it)l*iii*bro lucho logo(h*ii*igh
ga*ss ss*w*iii*rl*iii*ng *ii*in my thought fog
bubbled up my cave or foot the
wh*iii*s*s*tl*iii*ing knee and yr "towered
focu*ss*")*s*shoulder d*iii*m(III
walked *iii*n*ss*i*ii*de you burbled *ii*in the
*ss*h*ii*irt*ss* you wrapped yr arm*ss* a
round a bowl*ii*ing ball ju*ss*t a
*ss*hadow *ii*in the du*ss*t'*ss* broken
w*ii*indow *ss*i*ii*igh*ii*ing *ii*in the wall
~ ~ ~ ~ ~ ~ ~ ~ ~

"never walk aga*ii*in" the
T-*ss*h*ii*irt *ss*ta*ii*ined ah
beercan*ss* dr*ii*inki*ii*ing *ii*in
a ⌐ corner

...*goat paths*...
- C. Mehrl Bennett

olvido de la poesía

under the sweating corn your
plume .meal ,worms ,basinets
.a sog trunk ,wood .the
ball peen .pocket of hay the
.short seen ,toweling .my
massed dinner plates and
focal shifting ,porkid
peldaño do.nde el na
són .bluts angre ,meltid
aegypti in yr foggy len
tes ,lentos los dientes
se caen y me t.oco
el hígado .bruma d
onde .las manos spread
los labios rent las pie
rnas inacordadas como
bandoneón jodido
)*wandering the weathered*
form(

...in xochitl in cuicatl...
- Bernardino de Sahagún

olvido sin motivo
- *para Elvira Balcells y Martín Gubbins*

long steep mud so shiny seed
eye rocking on the drippy
counter son mis enojos vi
stos invis ibles tried to s
crawl the hill up my
brimming ≈ shoes sin pies ...
)eh sleep ,rising in my
hip ~(*numen wound* ...
)the throated suit tw
isted like ,a rope ,"polí
tico más ignor ante que
caca")perdón ,don Caca((
so I lay my dung to
s weep   *dreamed a storm*
sin motion

...el mar siempre parecerá el resto de un diluvio.
- Ignacio Balcells Eyquem

olvido del viaje

*mi tonelada mis cumbres mis
huesones aguados* ...entre
las tumbas tumbo ,sabor
de grava y orinas ,una
muralla verde sin ventana
con pinta **POE MAP E**
y ¿dónde la tormenta?
)my wheels shining in
the soup and laundry(
isofaction and a dense
)peso líquido ,foggy s
cales ,the whistling
road(my liquifaction
...simetría y foco es
trellado I couldn't
stand I stood I s
at I couldn't ...*sit
uation of yr fósil* a
hogado ,entro ,entre

las piedras • • • •

...gritty tooth...
- Dr. N. Ulo

olvido del reading

abjured the book nuts hubba
entries sleeping in your dawn
identity destroyed meat the
wet organs ejaculated in the
dust the chitter fiction white
pages pages black mouth
in the glossy religion naked
veterinarian backward skin
ah shot entelechy fields time
dies ellipse dis membered
root in the chill "maze of
ants" your eye sweat
read the metallic policy
script ,wings ,*hhaaiiirr*

...de todo escribí.
- Ivan Argüelles

*De scrito de "(sleeping madonna)"
de Ivan Argüelles*

olvido aritmétrico
  - for Bob Grumman

fil fils fin nor once the 1
nabbed outside my ½ eye
thawed in 2 the 3ice ¡o
nunca visto! mis 4mas
invisibles suben al 5nto
donde yo ,le fils de 6
palabras ,wallowed in my
7 X 7 books)I 8 no 7th air(
)*mosquito's sharp whine*(
9 strings quivering in
my ear el fin me
surge ,inindicado ,el
10 – 9 the 9's aspiration
was my "countless face
mirrored in your zer**O**"

...les pièces ils sont displacées.
- Marcel Duchamp

olvido del cacahoaquáhuitl

ruta o reloj mis cacasitas o
tliltic cacáhuatl foaming in
the back of my eye the other a
pool under stone where ,)*so
mething drib bles in my p ants(*
yr comb's teeth rustling in
my pocket "tines to go"
wheeling ,shouldered ,swimmy
,toenails in the ticking dust

,,, *...drew the bloody page*
my itch reissue ,protect the
shitting factor ,steep funct
ion zipping around in's
dark panting at the foot
of the bed the highway sh
rivels and *my headless
drink dries on the street*

...y a veces échalas en el agua...
- Fray Bernardino de Sahagún

olvido del olvido

went to fog phony sheeting
crashing off the walls no
studs just empty stone w
here the firey niche s pills
its tongue o inti mate mi hue
hueteotl giggling a escondidas
en mi gorra pulcra de
mocos y moscas ,my long
bent groan my .wind the
leg ,peldaño iztac ,wan
dered through the last b
lack closet ,my ent
ered chest ,interred ,wh
istle stopped ,more than
useless ,useful ,groping
through the daylight like
a fingernail .)) *plaster crum*
bled on the floor my
bed a gravelly strand...........

...ni mar ni mater...
- Antonio Machado

olvido playero

restless indication matters im
pactly foghorn ,focused ,f
aster blasting at the wall tus
hoyos inmanentes ,de azúcar
atestados ,tianguis en la ,pl
aya sumergida ,roofless
cloud hangars with their
blood-spattered walls rows
of legs nailed to the plas
ter dust caking on the
headlights what my active
hinges saw recounted ,m
uy estimado ,fíe en mí
.*I ran across the road I
swallowed all the keys I
stimulation crashed the
faucets gleaming in your
trunk* ,was saddled wit
h a suitcase ,standing
in the w,Wind

...mi costa nula, con túnel.
- Vicente Huidobro

olvido of the barking

hot loop saw)*fog ,lens ,comb*(I
shaped the defecation or my]long
mud walls[something yipping a
round the corner of my pocket
fishbones "saw" the thundered
time the years which ne *ver*
raining and the clump of hair e
merging from adobe where an **X**
was wrote)*circle blade flashing
in the sky*(I lay my crown en las
heces del patio tus lentes y
orinas toes squirming in the yell
ow mud saw sleeping on the
benches or were those books I
,remembered to forget ,hojas de
bbrruummaa and I was barking
without a sound ,behind the
hole where a door used to be

"Don't be a dog's bowels"
- Darby Conley

olvido del libro

my plunging soap uh ,pill piles ,p
ages or were they windows ,why the
matter's name's crowded halitosis

,wrought ,bent ,striation like a *f*
lag)*tomb barker*('less my
chamber floods and your darkest
drink streams through a hole
down hill ≈ ≈ .*the rodent
sleeps* and I my whisper dog
,chewing ,drizzled ,the stone's
thought inside ,kinda light
but gritty ,faceted ,bar
ely breathing as I watch th
at dimming wall of books th
ose hats in dust those shoes
strangled on their tongues
.*my soap sleeps in mud and
all your towels are drowned
,"blame your fingers"*

...*aguas negras*...
-Manuel Acuña

olvido de la tinta

ya looted ink **CRAW** nap said ,bas
ta !the tented legs my s wallow fis
ted sc**RAW**l a ,nostril song ,es
calera ,needles gargantescos ,wr
ITten with a file yr d ragging
soap cum**PUL**sion ,wheezing

every bite o yr **NO**dding
bullet pen soaking in the pall
id sugar of yr neck hay
golpes en la flooded TV ,vi

da ...lo sé ,*no* ,a**NO**tado co
mo nido los ,cuyes dormidos
y las piedras se deswaken
,pertas ,inex ...el son nar
igón o ,)máscara de aire the(
,))laundry tumbling down hill((
)))*río crashing in the stones*(((

...fabeto es, y crito...
- César Vallejo

olvido blessé

*puzzle ,knocking ,shot the shadow
,leg tribulation the ,fog shoulder*
dozes in ah ticky loop a whining
bites my arm)*sin permiso*(& yr
AK47 fulla mud .it's cramping
boulders in my suit why nu
mb er s yphilitic nozzle in
my clock you seethe ,dro
wsy ,drooling in my sleeves
.*aim* .*lock an cold* .)))blunted
swelling where the pillow flow
er fills with bees . . . . . .

...cada golpe lo conté.
- Lic. H. Umo

olvido del camino estancado

hoy **SOT** rings comprado he las
tumbas fists inacordados¡ alúm
brame !pancreatitus of the wallet
storm ,stone ,maybe mañana loo
se r twisting in my shuttered
circle ,why the neck why it's
asunto nulo ni aforkid prace
slu mber))((*yr docile*
hands rise the towers
burn)on the lago distant a
)sleeping boat)pescador del
aire)y la tarde)de humo
)dying sweat reverb)eration
)uh((((((( ][was
shut the door on shore was
chewing off the dollars was
wallowed in my bloated
esophagus ,stuffed with
pills a silbo de 5000
años que todavía suena
,suena intocado como agua
desaparecida que *re*
cuerdo que no recuerdo

Il faut boire la poussière.
- Arthur Rimbaud

olvido de la merienda

esencia rutailante ni nadedal
,combo plate scraped into yr
pants ay fog rising from tus cal
zones acacaoados ¡salud!
and grin into la bruma densa
de tu mano amocada

   '

write into the light and bring
)long sausage folded into
bun and(scalded window
leant against the wall my
sure belt lost oh trouser
index swell for me !)
rabbits lost around the
corner where yr shoe
lunch(bolder than
,twice impacted ,dar
ker than my blinding
lunch :I was you I
"thought" ~ ~

...vers...murailles...
- Francisco Quevedo, traduit par Isidore Ducasse

olvido salpicado

f**lap**ping an sh**in**ing the ch**urn**ing
g**ate** just one intensely liploid
como agronómico entered the g
runting stone – *its its* – rain
dreams me the adobe brick drips
mud ≈ dogs and shadow ~
yr mirror door peels back y
no ,inada ví ,*onada unada*
anada enada ynada ,señorita
,flama finiquita tus dedos
ajíes ~ ~)*ah ah*(-)my arms
are towels my face a shiv
ering fountain *play your*
leg like ammunition(crawling
across the sea like ants
"shining an flapping" ,*churning*
~)*your breath enters an egg*()

...besoin de urine.
Dr. T. O. Islet

olvido del cruce

ni inmigración ni inversión ni
perro con su lucro irrascible
,lo que yo infarto ,separo
,in ...risible pues ,ni modo

,fíjate O)*sin lentes*(O in
manente y el techo se
cubre de plumas y plomería
)*huesos y bolsas ,tremores*
y orinas bajo un
mesquite ,una botella
*vacía ,ni hormigas ,**cala***
vera ennegrecida por el
fuego ~ ~ (*un* SUV
sin ojos desaparece en el
polvo del río ~)*ni viento*
ni frontera ni nube aus
ente con su camisa de
zopilotes))un peso enterr
ado in aguantable((...si

,sí e**S** ...

...spit...(that eye)...the scratch...
-Edgar Allan Poe

olvido de la mancha

loot the thing glow nape fired wha
t yr chew leg yr sign nap aged
inside the corn ear worm my)sud
den show(s e e m s tous
led ,combinationed ,sudorífico y
...plough ,uh plow sieze uh sees
the shadowed lung collapsing in my
rainy suit the *chairs burning*
on the roof the knotted high
way yr eye the ashy lens
folded on yr moon clotting ,)ch
eese mouldered in a bowl(the
dusty ...blue stone ...splashing in t
he ink ✺   my
bushy recollection's shaking in's
breezed *blinks below the lake*
,wired ,and grew outside your
egg ...*zapateo intonso* ,sop
orífico y pensante un
logolvido .disuelto ,su
mo y fijo ,"*ni coche mor*
tífero"

...endomitis ,plumífero...
- Rubén Bonifaz Nuño

olvido de la mar

por temorizado na dado a pulcro
son ,mis dedos inpiesados)*fulgor
,túnel*(los ríos sincólicos no
llegan al mar ni la ,boca me
abren)pirámide de adobe la

playa ensombrece ▲≈(ay
cúspides la grava crunch ah
fork twisted like your leg
decapitation)*araña con ca
beza con tumi*(y levanto
la mano a mi boca sin b
oca a mis dientes indencionales
and I crave that snore c
arving skull 70 años sin
lengua :lo hablado soy mas
no lo dicho ,y espero la
playa de lodo ...*stu
mbling pelícano* ...sh
irtless an loud

...ondas...
-Anónimo

olvido de Byron
    "For in it lurks...",
    Lord Byron, *The Giaour,* 1813

nod focused lint on cliff he
belts the scorned bloody hand
the truly apeish smell invisible
to all but him scurrilous nape
dancing with lice's grave flash
of's unearthly wave's my
ass pyration cornered in the
much of times the glancer f
lopping in my trousers ah
nameless spell !the gazer
slept unspeakable and claims
the bird the sock puppet
met alone ,your pale lip
blister ghastly quivers
!yr swallowed birth dou
bles in that spitting doom
yr dribbling features vulgar
in the wading gloom

¡Quítate los lentes!
- Ramón López Velarde

olvido de Lara

lumpy ,his name forgot ,dan
dled ashes on's pate while
the others prate their hidden
lot gated with a smoky
door his silence blears
against the walking world's
hot mud his mirror his
fleshly worm clogged
those thrashing hoses on
his path bedecked with
stopsigns ,ladders ,c
loud giggling of that
secret glass that blood
passed outside what
oval time did start a
swarm of gnats bedecked
his skull a separate
head rotting off's
offending throne

"His madness was...sought..."
-Lord Byron, Lara, 1814

olvido ahogado

ay the dud shade blinks I
swam the cowed blade ff
lippping as it sinks *El Deca
pitador* my head's spoon re
plies the wwavess why do
ggy focus swallows the corn
or dunes pouring through the
windows ddryy wwatterr clau
sal sshakkingg rest all day re
treats into the hill's circled
stone)ddeadd eeyee(my plea
ding breeeezze my dull shape's
white blinding island

El lago te seca...
- José Asunción Silva

olvido del punto final

.jaw .ton .lop .mrate .fell
.blit .shell .apt .toad .nort
.chow .sog .flap .chase tore
.blangk .flab sort chain .cheese
.dream the lang fog .sweats
.ring time with sodden loot
.file .rain knot half business
stumbler note .bull .feel sat
behind shapeless politician rots noose
.drum .leak fold meat cloud
nods and flakes a .coughing
.dime muscled tooth yr tongue
stuck in sweet blood .slathered
.reached the fog watch ladder
rusting in weeds below the
.tower .the *tower* .*the towerrr*

...peluquería...
- Catulo

olvido del volante

no**d** ,focus at the dog hole lint ,luz

,morcilla ,nu**b**es antelúdicas ,el tornillo de tu pierna izquierda la tuerca de la derecha// *half bark*\\ wheezing on the roof your soaking shadow dries .the .leaning air ,bulemia sin matices el viento ,,,*dunes dragged across the desert*,,, that wad of nostril fuzz scraped the shape of earth the dripping sea *the whistling corn* ay cubo de as pirinas en llamas donde se empieza el tiempo ,bi-idílico ,chortled ,swearing and sw eating beneath the blistered wall | my troubled neck be

gins *my **d**ou**b**led neneck mmy*

...knifeedged disk...
- John M. Bennett

olvido pajarero

bull for**k** ladder him's the twosome
,soggy crash hidden in ,what
suit – pestered *'round the*
hats – mortífera la cumbre
ahogada the ,slumbered stairs
stars inhaled ,clawed force
,butyl wind coronado con
,tus mangas ,infladas ¡ah
was "*chewing up the rungs*"!
)*ornitología*(tongues and
sweats)*liposuction*(crushed
the buttons with's teeth and
,blew away ,efectivo ni bol
sillo - ¡nor my twisted
shoe ,bullet!)*bullet*(*like a*
toenail snagged inside yr
sock the sodden sleep the sleep
your other mist hid from you

...traje de...chorizo...
- *José Lezama Lima*

olvido del cadáver

tabled the loose storm the
sot cloud sought my sock res
tful bunching in my shoe oh
leafy pants twisting in the
breeze not yet .double singing
what .step .burned ?the chairs'
legs re versed the c lock wad
dles off ...my nestled drink
fulfillment ,stunning ,itch ,fork
ditch brimmed .ay what
doggy cirrus impaled !*my
tines bright with hair and
staples*)what jammed the
zipper(*where did this go?*
seated on the stairs ,no
dding ,slow drool ,my na
ked feet smeared with blood

...hormigas...
- Manuel Acuña

olvido olvidado

. bush . lunch . check . gristle
. plain ,growling the . ashpit
. leaf roof sore . bing . chafe
. sundered spit a . deck . pill
smear . shirtless fog . bin
time the . rot door blast
. bubble crap . torn . boot
. chewed the leaf . my ,floor
tomb . ambles root ,a bomb
. numbers in the . raw room
. where the drink tub .
.   .   .   .   . mist . peel .
. long water . was a
flood muzzle . mine . fu
lla light . where I . th
ink a . crust . sodden
under foot

...not...yet...
- Anónimo

olvido des serpents de la langue

comme des serpents since
prop goat tongue leurs ex
créments fly-value c'est
muet some meat sense
écrit sur la porte dorbb
puzzle les enfants qui
hurlent churm onto woun
ded screef fabrics to
morrow on dit le numéro
)washing dishes(a réparé
l'oubli word-made solvent
devant le parking watering
trash avec des plantes
l'agitation des lettres bag
feral diet that ellipse
de la logique noisy strings
de l'école)la fenêtre souple(
behavioral ganste traj
ectories les insectes voir
les yeux window fiction
airplanes complex transnatio
le papier à letters chats
imprimés world system
presque nuit dream identity
de l'abattre semi-autibio
de la crever fish around
on réclame la mort all that
stuff lost letters les
haines anciennes cycle

streets force less words
décès mains combats
dialogue forgotten publique
prison bats regime basks
dans nos bouches obvious
signatures gros mots cor
ner malade static re
sists chaos c'est rester
dans le noir eye books
tides anarchists mutter
un seul système il est
temps rubber cigaret fact
d'aller poison opens dormir
un peu :guts ,bank ,les
molécules d'eau alpha
bets tombent spelling
le monument à distance
mail ,dit ,trop tard
la rue les rêves *obvious
chain*

...rester dans la chair.
- John M. Bennett

*from Jim Leftwich, Six Months Aint No Sentence,
Book 28, Roanoke, Virginia, 2012
&
Frédérique Guétat-Liviani, Prières de.,
Barjols, [France]: Éditions Plaine Page, 2012*

olvido corriente

the *soup was glue* .tine unravel
,mesa disuelta ,rincón tubér
culo embadurnado por ende ,lo
que drank I ,lumbery down
the sidewalk ,acera aseverante
tus lúmenes surround that
pendejato thrashing on the
stage .your fog foot re
tracts folded in yr shoes
yr sweat stink ,foamy
biles ,sorta squeally
every paso ,pasos to ,ni
enfocado ,wiped yr butt
with a flag .the spoon
inmóvil ,cucharón y
cara tus lapbios que
jahabplan ni modo *some*
thing forested where yr
face once was somet
hing rivered where yr th
roat was ,twisting in
the rain ; ; ; ; ; ;

...ne laissent derrière elles que leurs
excréments.
- Fréderique Guétat-Liviani

olvido del fango

lovely stain la mancha cruda
camisa abierta como tumba
source of wind of clouded
breath the turds I reft be
hind a mattress fulla bro
ken watches and a listed in
ventario de cumbres y culos
rasca sin cielos the lake
drains away ≈ .....)surely
drippless ,the plunging knot ,re
focussed in yr throat where
gnats congeal ,a longer
clod retained ,yr exhal
ations ,gristle fist ,wh
at said the ,never ,spat
the buttons out whined
in time O O O(*crumbling*
chain ,buried in the thou
sands years)or just
my eye ,defocussed on
your rising mud

...lodo...y tripas...
- José Eustacio Rivera

olvido de la hora ciega

el pezón del sueño in
agotable error ur
ano en la luz del
paraguas nunca ví
las colmenas mudas
las brumas sin peso
ni dardos ,simposio ne
fasto la vulva es
pectral del mino
tauro bum bum mis
cuernos en la or
eja del tren dia
nesco paradero de
las montañas par
lanchines la leche
roja de los re
lojes del sal
)las hachas verdes
y antropófagas(

*Un ronroneo escuchado en
"(el pezón de Diana)" de
Ivan Argüelles*

olvido del right churn

right the churned tool locker
floats across the ,melted towel
,gas lever ,what I wondered
launder maze cow sings na
pped ah .lease an crash
,what learnèd drool forth the
swelling book brick all .ni
ght ,my dreamed socks my
.)))outer wind and a beach
of glass

...brisa...nula...
-Rubén Darío

olvido del fusil

plume high crack uh neck
faucet withered soon enough
,suerte de túnel por la
frente como si   .negate
the missle yawn the
doubled time redaction
what was spinning *was*
spinning y   .goteo nor
teño la cena servida
omni-intencional the
air retreats the snore

impales el humo "*K*"
escribe desescribe y
me quedo con la cueva
desdentada ,ay abierta
.el pulmón the motor the
sizzling clouds

...in yautli in huitztli.
- Cuauhtemoc

olvido teológico-político

*bed s**i**nk sh**i**rt* or)wall nacre(
must the ,melter foam r
unning out the cut-off heads
ah .estilation ,dug fog ,muck
filled with .hair your .meal
worm file what "thousand"
smile retained¡ oh nor n
ail !chewed the buttons off
,said uh "thinking dirt" your
face behind the skin 2

rising **S**nake**S** ,was blood
,was all was fake ,dusty
in the corn ,just still ,p
roudly blotted like your

heart b**u**rning in a bowl
)sheared right off ,the
peltless crowd ,shouting
for the *end of time* my(
useless jaw dangling

from a shel *f*

...huehueyetztli...
- Motecuhzoma

olvido del warehouse
   -for Mary Jo Bole

drainss an crowdss ,tonnag*ee* chancr*ee*
,*ss*hould*ee*r*ee*d *ss*law falling in th*ee*
*s*soup my r*ee*stiv*ee* l*ee*g com
paction pr*ee*ss*ss*ing on the wall
your plas*s*teer *ss*w*ee*at*ss* in ,th*ee*
rimlees*ss* pag*ee* you won th*ee*
talcum*ee*d dirt ah drooling
on th*ee* piggissh *ss*mok*ee ss*w
irling up th*ee ss*tr*eeee*t !*ss*
tool*ss* ampl*ee* h*ee*ap r*ee*join*ee*d

thee t**O**ileet war*ee*houss*ee*
*ss*t r*ee*ak*ee*d *ss*tack*ss* t*eeee*t*ee*r
into haz*ee* b*ee*n*ee*ath th*ee*
roof th*ee* corn*ee*r glow yr
*ss*andwich *ss*parkl*ee*ss *ee*n
thron*ee*d on a plas*s*tic ch
air *oh fluor*ee*ss*ee*nc*ee* !withdraw
your lip*ss* forg*ee*t your t*eeee*th !*

La chair fumée...
- Le Comte de Lautréamont

olvido del weather report

nod thunder soap(en**DE**ble)y
el viento fuerte(cúspide de
hormigas ,shadow swallow the
)whirring hands exfocused on
that bolus you received)*in
ched the corpse worm your
dragged beef business suf(*
fered the grimy shingles of
yr rain injection ,boca a
guada dientes de corales mu
ertos *es la infolemia* puk
ing the thickened insults s
ticky wax in yr ears la
borrasca muforma ,camisa
como ,flama tortugada and
I'm washing in my sleep ,de
qualified ,yes and yes a
gain the street aslosh with
words with sewer overflow
with hamsters chittering
on the steps   ⚡   >>

...laugh and drink your headache.
-don N. A. Die

olvido of the maggots

rusher clodt ah Club TV
chanted in the attic where
the basement floods the
ashy lake opens at your
door incomitante un
continente .swerve to
,war combiled ,the crashing
clouds beneath my desk
your streaming knees your
fabled suit of slice ba
loney Lip Smack Me !
in town the frantic mud
the snore inside your cake
it's shore mind turns
and "waves")what
tissue gashed with
slime reflection)*yr
plunging loot sticky and
legless ,shimmering with
fruit flies* ·····························((

...buzz cock sonata...
- Sex Pistols

olvido del universo

toast the gun bajo la en
ramada una canción flopping
mute sprawling in the mud
en dónde estamos el mundo
untouched quivers my floating
head ha cambiado de lugar
my crawling pants toward
your cordajes de guitarra
sobre el mar its swallowed
bullets its sombra ,es algo
que alza el vuelo toward the
coughing sky my ear junta
al arco voltaico says the
throne hole where un aero
plano daba vueltas my
letter lost against the sun y
en el aire un pañuelo de
textualized de focused ninguna
casa tenía puertas drinking
the air un lago oblicuo el
camino sobre thunder hace el
espacio el campo inverso
my fingers burning mañana
será el fin del universo

Entre los versos del "Universo"
de **Poemas árticos** *de Vicente Huidobro*

olvido calvo

Numbly dragged my
shirt my offal
cloud my lumber

Thought the sky
ham sweat
utter the under
growl weather
nor the lake

Insistance fold
,long tower
aimed into my
pocket where
the dirt lunch

Piled ,nor
source rabbit

All the **B**enches

Burnt the
asphalt seems

Vaciar tu cabellera sobre el mundo
- *Vicente Huidobro*

olvido del campanario du clocher

what the ham repealed a
cada son des cloches a
vein opens oiseaux de métal
the air flees ou donc est
tombée la primera canción
of the window a fart tous
les soirs a snore se enciende
a cada paso les yeux curtain
what cada hoja or quelque
chose your palms' nest a
bee palpita dans ta voix
that sliced thought those
teeth que mueren entre las
tejas your pants empty
sobre la lejanía

un reloj se vacía
- Vicente Huidobro

olvido de la casa de la maison

supper hurls sur la table
un abanico fluide no fork
left un oiseau muerto en
pleno vuelo like my eye or
leg la casa d'en face
white with blood
alguien pasea my hats
grow en el jardín ignoré
I never slept nor where
the humo se promène
brooms pour suivre el
camino you have to hay
que el faut recomenzar
spit in your pocket qui
a caché las llaves my
lip serviced finds just
tant de chose que no
pude encontrar

Se ha dormido...
- Vicente Huidobro

olvido de la colina

*sore flame hill my streaming
luggage emptied of its
watches un abrazo wr
iggles in the bathroom
where your pencil foams
like tulips where I clim
bed the crumbling slope a
door glass shatters
spilled my blinking
wine the stairs rise
to dark ah mattress
soaked with stars and
matches flame stutters
in your sock drawer
no hay billetera agarro
tada sólo una cabe
lleva inmiscible el cam
ino sueño blanco
la piedra negra te
sonríe a bird sin
alas te dice la
receta final ,la
que sigue*

I can't ... on.
- Samuel Beckett

olvido mortel

of saliva born del vacío tu
cabeza singing in the mud
la gran palabra the thread
of time el mar doble su
vida never again before la
enorme mano mouth like
a hospital que renace if
it has a name de sus
cenizas in mud la pal
abra olvidada the small
pane hissing alfabeto
perdido dank sections
of meat sobre las mon
tañas opposite the in
visible one como una
carta sections falling
la escalera de los
roof holes de la mu
erte glass sleep
de sus estatuas darning
socks dusty caminos
sin historia under the
door cuántos laber
intos mundos)ven
idos a menos cast
to sea ,en compañía

from Ivan Argüelles' "(mud)" 2012 &
Vicente Huidobro's "La Gran palabra" de
Poemas póstumos (II), en Obra poética, 2003.

olvido reversado
- para Luis Bravo

ap**es** toso mais le soleil se
abre the windows chime my
leg withers my mother's sm
all fox grins at the back of
my desk y abro "un" libro
son los vientos del túnel
*)running around( )la rue
atestada de los no(* si
me cago behind the d
oor loor de)nulo(
)lo(densativo rein
versado deinversionante
versus that thick shoe

swallowed **step up** the
anteimustio mis pan
taleones incrustados de
la cita folderol – *in the
room filled with leaves*

Odio la poesía.
- John M. Bennett

olvido del colmo

trained loquacious sanding
off my tongue it's yours
.toweling labia an nor lastre
indomable tus nojones run
dementales so aimless I
or eye lacustre)*no*
dder shape( )*lente*
cato(fromage in
editable sweating un
der the flies and
saddled the thorny
bush .)*m,y ,d,r,i,b,,,,*
,b,l,i,n,g,,,)interbation ,f
restive lunng shirdt I
couldn't stobstart talg
king ay he dicho
.)*red mask deep be*
neath my dusty feet(((.

...coughing...
- G. R. Unte

olvido de l'allée

*l*ong *l*evered headache storm
lintgrown chair speeding tow
ard the foggy screen the
foggy shade slapping on the
glass your tiny dirt half
lunged shadow towel dri
bbling in the ink your len
til soup contained ah ha
lf uh ,morty shorts ,a
balone glinting in the
toilet where yr belt
se ahogaba a light
pole sweats outside the
window *ss sss ssss*
chew your leg an iso
lation crisped inside yr
shoe its tumba corn
its looted teeth drowned

in oil and hair your ha **t**

growing rai n ; ; ; ; **N**

...respiro la calle orinosa...
- Leopoldo Lugones

olvido del ojo

the cheese neck ,hOwling curd
where my stapled laundry turned
below the bed a hose dancing ,lay
ered in the glinting room *gleaming
in the smoky corner* where a
mask is stacked on toilet paper
:injecta claw ,peeing on the
book: *the long fog grease time*

)why shirty(**heavy boat ha**
lf sunk you raise your head
whey ,*doubled doubting* ro
amed across the clear lint
clot o peeling nose the
feet crowd my gated
wander burned my swal
lowed head)*your rat key*(
where I saw the skull be
decked with flowers
,dark and crumbling like
my hands)lost in
seeing ,the tabled word

burnt

...ixpopoyotl...
- Huitzilopochtli

olvido del boy scout

uh haw ,yout mate ,treble
shapes or blind clubbage round
about the mothy chairs the
spurting heads filed teeth ch
unks of pinky brain)*lung
time*(:the rat snore ladder
,*twaddle*: mutely blaring at
the slime shining on the
walls))*yeah ,sure ,flame
it off*((tossed the wind
ow out the perciatelli
whistling ,*w i n d*
inchy creep of bowls my
blood)nostril(apetitosa
apt to *cringe* knotty
nodding like langosta d
ropped into ah thrashing
boil *¡oh form gristle
itch for me!*)*where
the glass once stood* ,a
dusty form................ . . . . .

...bugger...foot...
-William S. Burroughs

olvido del pozo

y*um*my ash yes ,andomino
,polenta rica del riñón mis
whistles crowder ,bleating
dog*ggg* haploid dip inside
yr "cone")of apetito(st

rain upon the flushing **b**

owl)wheeling ,wh*eeee*ling(
empirical el fogonazo s
lick off uh tongue your
soap dinner pito *what*
yr shadow boiled a "non
sense nuisance" ,*mirror*
into space your itchy
fork spreading tine
and gnats)your lint
faucet cries,, , , , ,(

La piedra sin forma...
-Federico García lorca

olvido de la obra

n*i* engarglantado n*i* enso
bado ni mis güevitos sur
cacados con los riañosos a
güitas emplapados supe no
supe la nadacosa floppy
beneats my sleat sp
adtered with a día realita
)apbrí la broca y la pa
labrabla me manchoseaba
la cramisa oronta...(
≈*onda lapsus*≈ fraught
whis ker b ,eating the
sheet gargabateada ay
me perdí el tomotambo
los bloquelibros caídos
al ≈*río*≈ turburbujlencia que
va que vaviene ni vaivén
de mis plumas ahogadas
ni pajinal de esta blo
ombing on my desk ni

f*i*n *i*n*i*nf*i*n*i*to

Obras completas...
- Augusto Monterroso

olvido del cuate viento

sucker neck the gland
ulular de mis abuelos la
loose grinning in the
hay con bosta filled
but's just palabras son
,poemas)nada(si
lencios where no sil
encio srounds .)*my*
fog-draped leg my
louder cheek half
storming out the room(
~→   ~→   ~→

~ ~ ~

-Ehecatl

olvido of the blind

soli d *UNI*tario .meseta .in
tensiva la ,pleni luna del
fork "fatuo" es .raw t
rowel its blood its drip re
hearsal or .donut cage
the .s.an.d ri.se.n a.g
.ainst t.he .gl.ass .ah
buried dog and robe !cor
onta y pechero *.oro del*
hueso y .huata sin piel
sin .desayuno .lesser
change en .ters m
.y figuración *fi.gúr*
ate .**no** .**simón** ."el
desierto de mi lengua"
)))se)))))seca en el mar

.... 🌀 ....

...lo ciego que ví.
- Alonso de Ercilla y Zúñiga

olvido de la manguera

"the" "ch **O**pping fl**OO**d" flidd
les gummy soup shoulder wawa's
chest ,rotting birds a nest
glass burst the hammy
water y las soledades
al revés "plenty too
thy" *jáhaw a'jaw*)the
mask clutched to's("y
et archive"   .the wind boul
der ,sp lashing air I .was ne
kkid inside my shirt you
.)*plunger at the gate*(
raised the bowl oh ch

alchihuite !)wet st**O**rm

st **O**ne ,de la barriga
llena ,grava ,o se
millas del reloj que
masticaba la carret
era de torturmenta de
mi lábpiz flojo "sp
raying ink like a hose ≈ ≈ ≈ "

...n'écrit rien.
- Samuel Beckett

olvido del menudo

tool the hatted air mon
coin t'estimule ay el dedazo
que a mí el ojo arranca ,*el
izquierdo* ,the normous head
dimmer than a cloud it was
n't "me" *it was me* at the
hammered box el trono de
tuercas ,cantinflando el
poema preciosísimo)*de
ciosidades*(y cojines em
papados de ruiorinas *the
)silvered hair*( )]insect tictic
king in the wall[('''''''''''''
' ' '   '   ' ''''''''''   ' '''   ''' '''

))...dropped my tdime in the draining
p**o**o**l...((

*...sommes noirs au miroir
de la guerre intestine*
- Jacques Dupin

olvido del cumpleaños

insufrido peldaño y)mucho riesgo

,m▪/▪◐(muerto ,summer clouds

,what brrreaks inside my hair uh
,70 nickels 70 long turds d
ropping in the crowded lake
,de ojos de ,pulmones thick
with lint ...)*the 70 shivers*
,the 70 wigs wall the 70
waves of linguini cooked
last week and(a neck
that never stops itching
,the 70 dimes you crawled do
wn to the sótano con sus
grillos)*70*(y libros '
)*70 x 70*(y your '
70 eyes gag the '
burbly floor drain '
your)boleto's thin '
smile spattered at the '
edge ' ,◉ ' ' , ' ' ,,, '

Soixant-dix les tombeaux de la boue.
- *Julio C. Tello, tr. de F. Ango Secco*

olvido del jamón

loot *SO* the sooty ham sock the
step burnt wandered off the chain
not livered numb ,nor too .said
the slab mite time re ignorited
)*blind log asleep in's light*(so's
the meat cut ,the mustard)*g*
as rising to the ceiling lamp(
))*dusty table through the win*
dow seen a hand without
its fork wall streaked and
dangles a crumpled photo((

)))*forget your shoes...*

...la lluvia de las caderas.
- Ivan Argüelles

olvido de la barranca

my bust	hat pool
swilling	the thunder
dog feet	wet gristle
grimy heel	your snore
pillow's stink	open my seen
wallow in hair	brine collapse
twenty thumbs	one lost
the cough	the neck
uh uh	sour kitchen
dung & light	mist tower
slow wrist	white & hung
blistered flower	um um
check the	off the
lost lung	numb plenty
relapsed time	thin glare swallowed
bean my throat	thinks mildew
spore door	feel slimy
whistle's met	meat fog
under the	spilling
drooled rat	just dry

The Same
- John M. Bennett

olvido del jején

"***do***g's lunch pile" yes dust
throne's grunt ,ahead's mute
soil's)bled watch(o)t
rot(never always ,not
)no(steam fading above
the stone flies rinsing wha
t mmy wwallow ed fflag
chchest)nester(wag yr
)mile a mile(a why I'm
seated dry a pool nom de
chair affreuse ,combien?
j'ai mangé los cero
tes "mágicos" ,blis
tered like my gusanito ay
gluglu ano andante "y
es")upper in the th
r o a t *u n   r*
e

...suello...pul...cro...
- Gabriel García Márquez

olvido de leftwich

the globe's paragraph swivelled
haunted gourd bla my leeched
suit crowned .talking dorks
support ,all the crested lath
burning in your phones your
turtle secretions ,turning a
living .instruments of false
tical erv ntial lacquer
hope completed develo the
swallowed laundry drying
on the desert coast th
)*inking cities*(in the ax's
roof or root .my blocked
ají on the border's grid
lock cancer where your
brimming thumb library's
beached among the cows
ay the "civilized" ,the
"spells" ,clueless fields
braying in the package
picnics...)"*looting the
junkyard*"(

the name s
- Jim Leftwich, Six Months Aint No Sentence,
Book 29, 2012

olvido de las tijeras

laundered and glummy .uh
nek ,trowel .fort of sh
ow plume ,e e e e e e e
.the sloshing shirt remem
bered forgot ,uh huaca
del aire .sieze .the .nail
traduzco inti-nada ,ah
charmed sore ¡blink b
read when ,oy ¡- - -
- - - - - - or scis ><
ors crossed ,outside
the fly the fly gate
π * * *

...y pateó la máquina.
- Sr. Ek

olvido del garrote

NO ,ya .palaver spilletd
nor whater should nig h
ni nada ,whap it up
the river shoots the
snore *fingers* ,torqued
molto and the skin
whistles ,glistens and
your eating)spoke
inside the itching
foot(ay bummer
face ,croissant the
streams of air)la
poesía que don nadie
lee(un pedo un
trueno un sortilegio
de ventanas ☐ ☐ vacías

...ejecución somera...
- Augusto Pinochet

olvido cumpleañero

the *sh*ore labelled crasher hailed in
denture came the fraught temple sp
lit in 2 or 3 .soap thumb and
force induction ,where I fell into
the bush .wet my shades I did
,why the dribble fell I crept
ashiver up the lawn .plastic gnomes
facedown in the mud .the door re
belled the clouds stretched dry the
hash was mailed in a sandwich
bag .

aimed and flamed the pawed con
"jecture"...

...por la caca, un trueno.
-Al Caparra

olvido of the deadline

"why whey wiggles" "it's
the name" "plutocrat")sharper
and leaking( )stare ahead
the glowing cheese("my"
)bomb(collapse "and
shower")beneath the huaca
invisible(_____ tower of
eyes "not the same")nor(
esenervencia)colder heels(
)and my ca(sh "choked
off" "mildewed sandwich
on my head" I)left
your "dreaming corn"(

...cansancio infinito...
- Jorge Luis Borges

olvido del cambio idéntico
-for Blaster Al Ackerman

aim the stroke of dung sword
rusting in the **be**d springs like a
hamster)water ≈ *could I guess(*
the fecal blade streams ≈ ~ ~ ~
)bark-faced lumber corn("etched"
in))~*fog*~((kinda like I s
lept and dreamed a greasy door
)*it was ankle heavy*(woody
flying with its hair of worms
)"mejor para la tos"(su sup
uración tomada ,acostada ,)dorm
ida *&&&* ...( ))"*all diffe
rent all the same*"((...y yo
que lo veo y no tengo nada
que ver

The Spitter in the lake...
- John M. Bennett

olvido del sponge mirror

ni reflejo pienso smoke wr
eaths the garage and all my
combs ..... ~~~~~ free of t
eeth the beard inhaled and
.......*ggone*~ ~ ~   )steaming in
the woods(~ ~ *la milpa se*
creta............./ / / / / ....
....................../ / / / /....................
y "yo" ,al revés ,me a
cuerdo olvidado ,en la
boca ,a glass ....\ \ \ \ \ \............

...ombres de maíz...
- Miguel Angel Asturias

olvido y fragmentos

seen each thing
the gnat
the plow
the lint

the saggy plumber
the thought dog gland
debt ,)and doubt(

mutter
matter
madre
)mute(

mood stool
my heaping throat
)tongue creel(

slaw ,hammer ,phone
knot leg
him

lumen nostril
sot
the dot half

no mute sand
"swallow the peeled sore"
"glag"

roof mildew law
huff it the
double wave
))muddy toast((

the mildewed raft
the rippling roof
)flat wind crime(

gawk
tub
mud
"sweater"

shine

swelling dork
the master swats
the spoon the flojo

nude ,tezontle
dime ,))maybe flood

oztli
hocker zoot
"loud socks"

the templo mullet
ran ,ni nada
"¡ay humito blade!"

mot dodder
aspirina
gasolina
unu

gnaw the soap
the spill the
thing
the slab

,rug ,snot ,leg
murder in the chert
tongue

lock the boot
mi cagado
)*stink mirror*(

olvido of the ashes

leak the singing SNore off yr
red skull lint my growling
combination floor yr)*a.s.h*
j.a.r( )under the corner sh
orts(yr fridge stuffed
with gristle and a hat
your teething your squalling
your pencil faster meatless
eyeball infibulation crawl
seeping down my jaw
)sticky with the leaves)yo
u)otro)tiburón vestido de
vaso trizado so I played
my thinning wig ,*tried*
to sleep but slept ,when the
sidewalk tunnels the
swamp)thinking
in the bony ear((((

...algo dijo.
- Petrus Borel.

olvido du dictionnaire

chew half the / cash rustle ,si
lent within the lint / your crea
med cage ,greased beneath yr
chair a corner of the galax /
y es "hora" que / nunca /
fluida ,liquen y spreading
thru the / hop thought my
/)safe resisdance( )*keeps
crawling*("I grew the raft"
pal / avered hours ,always
costly /)*with the padlocks*(
)where yr suited finger "b

right with" blood... / ,,,(

...resistance...
- Denis Diderot

olvido del cinderblock

your finger hummer's ,lake con
crete ,soc ked salami where yr
shoes switch flapping)I ,uh
glommed the do nuts shre
dded in yr)cilia what the
body surface swills ,a
]*door*[ )e las tic(...*m.i.s.t*...
))falling off the *light* switch es

...bug...spiral...
- Michael Dec

Includes some pellets found in
Michael Dec's "Surface Deucy"

olvido

the leaking pen)*sink*(t
ossed the bone scraw led t
ootoot -------------------------
)*maricas ,maricones*...( )*bowl y
ano*(año de mis túneles de
tectivescos on ,the table yr

fork **burns**)I swore in
side my "pants" be neath
the stacked stones ay t
hose cracking flags behind
mi asma o ¿son mis ojos
pretéritos?)*pedernales pretuer
cos preeternizados*(and I eat a

te - will eating? - that **stink**
"water in my spine" a

boom a cob a blot a *mil
dew crowned with shit*

...los poetas ahumados.
- Roberto Bolaño

olvido del fin

chub h**ash**er ,bones 'n all ni
modo la estructura que "co
memos y echamos" con las
mi gas)*thoughtless sea*(
was coughing on the beach
or)breathed into you(*scr
um plastic bottles styro ch
unks tam pon t ubes a
rub ber fli pflop mapa
mundi and my linty
face asleep behind "2
masks" in tlilli in tla
palli just fry 'em up*

...eating the end...
- JJohn M. BBennett

olvido del tambo

el fango de añ**os** me ,conta
minación wursteña y en el
cielo mi sombra condensada
)*l'ombre de nom*( )silly really(
tosudo y tonsilectomigajado
)*coughing*( )sinks in "water" o es
¿ruorina?≈(en el lixo mis
manos tango y al lado de la
caminada duermo ,inintimist
o ¿cómo me llamo? a swarming
in the garbage can a night
of drying bees a)*day inhabits*(
and I was "eating lunch" I
)*thought*(,el chorizo goteando
sangre≈ ,o agua≈ del pan o
,*ventanas abejadas que*
abro y abro

...que habla por la piedra.
- Neftalí Reyes

olvido del calor

sweater lung my fried dehousing

s ham "b**ir**ther" incompacted o
my leg restriction !I ate your
each was your "howling" giggle

ha flopping beneath the Chair ,ay
my egg impaction !)"*huevos*"
sleeping on your ,facial re
construction or the fault of
earth)*the hat half dries*(
)my hot mask lint my(fogg
ed eyes stre))))))))))))aming in the~
clouds ~ ~ ~ ~ ~ ~ ~ ~   ~   ~   ~   ~

Piramidal, funesta...
- Juana Inés de Asbaje y Ramírez de Santillana

olvido dull end

es

¿Puedo irme ahora?
- Felipe Cussen

olvido raining

ee**N e**el *"rreeiinnoo"* eentrréé ,s

iinn p *iiees siinn loo ii*m*pacta*nn*tee ee*l
)*"eeseennciia" dee loos* pul*crroos
zapatoos p*eerr*diidoos een* la
*coorriica*nn*cha d*ee *mii cuarrtoo dee*(
*ba*ññ*oo iimpalpablee "shiimmeerrii*nn*g
wiith liight eerrs"* y m*ee habl*óó *ee*l
*lavaboo ,coo*nn *u*nn*a lee*nn*gua dee
hulee* y la *rreesoo*nn*a*nn*ciia dee*l
*cuboo dee cabeezas deeseechadas
doo*nn*dee* la *pueenntee ee*nn *ee*l

*deesiieerrtoo ee*nn*trraba* 干 ....
)my mask II w*oorree ,oo*
u*nn*dula*nn*t
*oo*nn*ee ,*nn*ameed acrrooss ,thee*(
poost- deel *a*nn*t- dee"iièèrree"* la
*coorroo*nn*a dee mii culoo ,*nn*a)lgaas
diiseecadas quee beeséé ee*n *ee*l
alta*rr* dee)*humiitas ,deel humoo*nn*doo
,*y *dee*l *toos reetrrooactiivoo ee*nn *mii
caja dee a.i.i.i..r.r.r.e.e.e*........................

...I was always...not...
- John M. Bennett

John M. Bennett's OLVIDOS

John M. Bennett may well be the *avant* in avant-garde when it comes to contemporary American poetry. Straddling 2 centuries now of constantly itching nouveau "everything" in experimental and visual poetry, Bennett has been at the forefront through various means: in the latter half of the 20th century with his *Lost and Found Times*, one of the great "small press poetry rags" of all time, and then through his Luna Bisonte Prods press. He has also been a fomenter and a collaborator with numerous other experimental poets. OLVIDOS ("Memories"; though the word also and literally means "things forgotten") is quite possibly his masterpiece. 339 pages of zany often inarticulate expositions of a kind of lunar madness that can only be the work of the descendent of such poets as Vicente Huidobro and Guillaume Apollinaire. OLVIDOS is characterized by impressive multilingual multidiacritical punctuational and multidizzying techniques that often leave the reader questioning not only his sanity but his vision. One might ask: are "Olvidos" a new poetry "form"? Certainly the many typo- and orthographical innovations point in that direction. A large number of the poems conclude with faux quotes, and some real ones, from many poets, mostly Latin American, which may place this work in the category of literary hoaxes. It is probably more accurate to align it with the intellectual slight of hand of Jorge Luis Borges, however. There is most likely something for everyone here from minimalist visual techniques and this zen-like "koan" :

olvido del moon

laundered sleep
test sink

to the neatly architectured poems such as "olvidos y fragmentos" with its enigmatic phrase "lock the boot". But then the entire text is one immense sequence of enigmatic and puzzling dicta, summed up best in his own portmanteau word "hablacagada". This is an important work and should place Bennett centrally on the map of great, innovative American poets.

Ivan Argüelles

www.ingramcontent.com/pod-product-compliance
Lightning Source LLC
Chambersburg PA
CBHW060552230426
43670CB00011B/1790